A Guide to
PORT SUNLIGHT
VILLAGE

Edward Hubbard & Michael Shippobottom

A Guide to
PORT SUNLIGHT
VILLAGE

including two tours of the village

LIVERPOOL UNIVERSITY PRESS

First published 1988 by
Liverpool University Press,
Senate House, Liverpool, L69 3BX

Reprinted, with corrections and amendments, 1990, 1996
and 1998
Reprinted 2000

British Library Cataloguing-in-Publication Data

Hubbard, Edward
  A Guide to Port Sunlight village including two tours of the
  village.
  1. (Metropolitan County) Merseyside. Port Sunlight, history
  I. Title   II. Shippobottom, Michael
  942.7'51

ISBN 0-85323-116-8

Set in 11/12 pt Palatino by
Wilmaset Ltd, Birkenhead, Merseyside
Printed and bound in the UK by
The Alden Press, Oxford

Contents

Front Cover: Leverhulme Memorial (see pp. 20–21, 59).
Back Cover: The Diamond (T. Raffles Davison, Port Sunlight, 1916, pl. 2) (see pp. 12–23 *passim*, 27,38, 57–61 *passim*).

Foreword

This guide is based on the same writers' Architecture section of the Catalogue which accompanied the Exhibition *Lord Leverhulme*, presented at the Royal Academy by Unilever in 1980 to mark their Golden Jubilee. With the consent of Unilever PLC passages from the Catalogue are here re-used. Reference may be made to it for details of sources, further Port Sunlight minutiae and consideration of Lord Leverhulme's architectural patronage as a whole, as well as for expert coverage of aspects of his collection.

The present work has also drawn on *The Buildings of England: Cheshire*, by Nikolaus Pevsner and Edward Hubbard, 1971.

Unless otherwise stated, photographs are reproduced by courtesy of UML Ltd or National Museums & Galleries on Merseyside.

Mr Edward Morris of the National Museums & Galleries on Merseyside, at whose suggestion the guide was undertaken, has given assistance, encouragement and advice. At Port Sunlight help was received from Mr P. K. Hodson (Estates Manager), Mr M. C. Moore (Head of Information Services) and Miss Ailsa Bowers (Information Officer) all of UML Ltd. Thanks are due also to Miss Maureen Staniforth, Librarian and Information Officer at Unilever House.

Preface

When I first joined the staff of the Walker Art Gallery in 1966, the largest room in the Gallery was entirely devoted to an enormous model showing the future shape of Liverpool city centre. Few then doubted the wisdom of the City Planning Department, displayed in the colossal rectangular slabs of this vast and visionary model. Already, however, Edward Hubbard was meticulously cataloguing the historic buildings of Merseyside and beyond for Pevsner's *Buildings of England* volumes, and, under the auspices of the Victorian Society, the Liverpool Heritage Bureau, Diocesan Advisory Committees and other bodies, he was describing their beauties and defending their continued existence. His facts were always correct, his tone always measured and his grasp of planning law never doubted. His scholarship was, however, ultimately more influential than his advocacy because the new concern for conservation of the last twenty-five years was primarily caused by public opinion, informed by a new generation of well-researched and intellectually stimulating architectural guide books. This is the last of those guide books to which he contributed. In it he and Michael Shippobottom describe, paradoxically, a comprehensive redevelopment scheme, engineered by an autocrat with powers unequalled even by a modern planning officer. But Edward Hubbard greatly admired William Hesketh Lever; it would be impossible to imagine two more different men, but both shared a humanity in their approach to architecture and a sensitivity in their appreciation of buildings which this book amply demonstrates—and which is the cause of the pride I feel in having commissioned it nine years ago.

Edward Morris
1996

ONE

The Founder

Fig. 1 Lever making a speech, in The Diamond at Port Sunlight, 1917, on the occasion of his elevation to the peerage

William Hesketh Lever (1851–1925) was born in Bolton, the son of a successful wholesale grocer, and with a family background of Liberalism, Nonconformity and abstinence. At sixteen he entered the family firm, became a partner at twenty-one and soon expanded the already prosperous business beyond the confines of Bolton. In 1884 he began to specialise in one aspect of the grocery trade, namely the marketing of soap. Sold under the registered name 'Sunlight', it initially was made to his formula by various manufacturers, but the following year he founded the firm of Lever Brothers to make it independently. A factory

was leased at Warrington, where production began in 1886. Despite this partnership with his brother James Darcy Lever (1854–1910), it is the powerful personality of W. H. Lever which dominates the story of Port Sunlight and the company.

Sunlight Soap differed from most current types in its superior ingredients, containing no silicate of soda and with more vegetable oil than tallow. Also—and this a notable innovation—it was sold neatly packaged and stamped with its name. Business was boosted by efficient salesmanship and advertising, the scale of which expanded over the years,

Fig. 2.   Housing replaced at Port Sunlight. Dwellings as squalid as many an industrial slum occupied part of the village's marshland site. Duke of York Cottages, Brook Street and the foot of Primrose Hill now occupy this area. Photograph early or mid-1890s

revealing Lever's seldom erring flair for astute publicity. With production having quickly risen from twenty to four-hundred-and-fifty tons of soap a week, new premises became necessary and in 1888 construction of the works at Port Sunlight was begun. The enterprise steadily grew and so did Lever's personal wealth; from early on, expansion was international in scope; it was accompanied by the taking over of, and amalgamation with, other concerns, and a policy of gaining control over the supply of raw materials was pursued. Multiplicity of business (including the development of margarine manufacture) led, after the Great War, to the moving of headquarters from Port Sunlight to London, and in 1930 Lever Brothers and the Dutch Margarine-Union merged to form the Unilever organisation.

The success of the early venture resulted in extension and alteration at the Warrington factory, the local architect William Owen being responsible. Owen received much subsequent employment from Lever and was involved in the creation of Port Sunlight, once it had become clear that the Warrington plant and its restricted site would have to be abandoned. Prompted by squalor seen in industrial Britain (Fig. 2) and by the social conscience which family background had engendered, Lever was determined from the first that a new factory would be accompanied by model housing for employees.

Next to business, Lever's chief interest in life was architecture; he actively involved himself in the development of Port Sunlight village and worked in close collaboration with architects employed both there and elsewhere. Countless construction and planning schemes reflect his own visual tastes, as did the art collection which filled several of his own houses as well as the Lady Lever Art Gallery. Building was for him an end in itself and he spoke of his enthusiasm when addressing the Architectural Association in 1902. Between marriage in 1874 and his death he occupied

Fig. 3 Lady Lever Art Gallery. 'Kent' Room, with fittings of *c.* 1730 from a house at Chatham

thirteen houses in total, each of which he either built or to some extent either altered or enlarged. This passion was expressed in special doors and chimneypieces introduced into the simple house in Bolton where he first lived after marriage, no less than in successive rebuildings, remodellings and extensions at Thornton Manor on his Wirral rural estate.

Concern for architecture and planning motivated many of Lever's public benefactions, not least the gift to the nation of the great London palace of Stafford House, renamed Lancaster House at his wish. Instigated by Professor (Sir) Charles H. Reilly, he developed patronly interest in the Liverpool University School of Architecture, and of £91,000 libel damages awarded against the *Daily Mail* and other newspapers, *c.* 1907, some was devoted to saving from demolition Liverpool's 18th-century former Blue Coat School, and the remainder was donated to the university, in part to establish a Chair of Civic Design—a then pioneering ven-

ture. In Bolton he bought and restored the historic Hall-i'-th'-Wood, presenting it to the town as a museum; a sumptuous Congregational church was built at the expense of his brother and himself; he initiated the erection of new, unified premises for Bolton School and gave a public park to the town, though attempts to promote schemes of town planning and civic improvement came to nothing. At Rivington, not far away, he formed another public park and built a re-creation of the mediaeval Liverpool Castle beside one of Liverpool's Rivington Reservoirs. Rather than being a folly, this had serious didactic purpose, no less than had the opening of Rivington Hall as a museum and art gallery. Comparable in educational intent were 'period' rooms at the Lady Lever Art Gallery (Fig. 3) and the use of Hall-i'-th'-Wood as what amounted to an early instance of a folk museum.

'Altering the face of nature was with him a

passion,'[1] wrote Lever's son, and his imagination was stirred by the challenge of Port Sunlight's unpromising site. (See p.9). On the large agricultural estate which he amassed in Wirral, not only was the village of Thornton Hough embellished and largely rebuilt as a rural Port Sunlight, but some five miles of avenues were planted. With the landscape architect Thomas H. Mawson, Lever laid out spectacular gardens at Thornton Manor, at The Hill (his London home at Hampstead) and at Rivington. On the bleak moorland hillside of Rivington Pike, at the edge of the Pennines and high above the reservoirs and the park, was built The Bungalow (or Roynton Cottage), commanding stupendous views and set amidst acres of lawns, terraces, loggias and lakes, all formed on the precipitous and inhospitable slopes. The first house there was burnt by a suffragette and its successor demolished by Liverpool Corporation.

Interests and tastes must have received guidance and impetus from the social contact which was maintained with architects, particularly Jonathan Simpson, a life-long friend. Stylistically, Lever's outlook was that of the late phase of historicism and, uncommitted to any theory or philosophy of architecture, his taste was eclectic. Generally he favoured classical interiors, but was disposed towards the 'Old English' of vernacular and Elizabethan revivalism and greatly admired the timber-framing of north-west England. Quality of materials and craftsmanship and perfection of detail are hallmarks of Lever's building, and are no less characteristic of him than are the boldness and breadth of vision which inspired Port Sunlight and the great gardens. Though he favoured grand formal planning, Lever's taste in classical architecture was for academic refinement rather than heavy Baroque.

The company's concerns overseas engaged his attention and he took direct interest in the design of factories, and in the planning of model settlements for native workers on Lever Brothers' plantations in the Belgian Congo.

Lever was created a baronet in 1911 and a baron in 1917, when he took the maiden name of his late wife Elizabeth Hulme to form the title Leverhulme. She had been a childhood friend, and was apparently a person of simple tastes and easy-going nature—the perfect foil for her ambitious, energetic husband. She died in 1913, having been Lady Lever, but never Lady Leverhulme. Hence the name of the art gallery which is her memorial. In 1922 Lord Leverhulme was raised in the peerage to the rank of viscount.

Dictatorial and vain, but astonishingly generous, Lever was a man of contradiction and paradox. Ruthless tycoon and autocrat, patron and philanthropist, the magnificence of his residences belied ascetic personal habits. He enjoyed a placid family life and a flamboyant public and commercial career generously punctuated with drama and incident—business warfare, the *Daily Mail* libel action and other litigation, the burning of Roynton Cottage, his mutilation of an Augustus John portrait and, at the end of his life, costly and abortive schemes for improvement and development of the Outer Hebridean Isles of Lewis and Harris.

This complex and many-sided genius remained a Congregationalist, a Gladstonian Liberal (representing Wirral in Parliament 1906–09) and, above all, a fervent disciple of Smilesian self-help. Attesting to wide reading and careful thought, his business philosophies and ideas on housing, planning and related social issues were expounded in numerous lectures and published addresses, as well as in less formal speeches. (Fig.1).

Though maintaining he always acted only for sound business reasons, the happiness and well-being of the ordinary man were genuinely close to his heart. In avowed spirit of enlightened self-interest, Lever sought to improve working conditions in industry, displaying humanitarianism, albeit with what would today be an impossible degree of paternalism. He introduced shorter working hours and benefit and welfare schemes and provisions, and in 1909 the plan of employees' Co-Partnership in Lever Brothers was established. Direct profit sharing was eschewed, and the creation of Port Sunlight and its communal facilities was the prime instance of what, in seeking a healthy and contented workforce, Lever termed 'prosperity sharing'.

NOTE

1 Viscount Leverhulme, *Viscount Leverhulme by his Son,* 1927, p. 86.

TWO

Background

At Port Sunlight two separate traditions in the history of town planning met for the first time. On the one hand there was the picturesque visual tradition derived from 18th-century landscape design as translated into the semi-urban terms of Nash's Regent's Park and the Regency suburbs, spas and watering places, with their villas and terraces in silvan settings. This tradition, with townscape subservient to landscape, flourished in Victorian times. It guided the planning of resorts such as Bournemouth and Torquay, and inspired countless well-to-do suburbs, with curving tree-lined roads, in London and the expanding industrial towns and cities. The ideal was continued in the influential Bedford Park, at Turnham Green, begun in 1875 as a self-consciously 'aesthetic' middle-class 'garden suburb', with from 1877 work by Norman Shaw.

The other tradition—a social one—was that of materially decent conditions for the urban working classes. The movement for housing and sanitary reform, dating from the 1840s, included Sir Edwin Chadwick, Lord Shaftesbury, Samuel Peabody and Octavia Hill among its campaigners, and the 1851 Housing and 1875 Health Acts among its achievements. The special movement for the provision by individual industrialists of housing and social amenities in connection with their factories may be traced back to such schemes as Richard Arkwright's village at Cromford, Derbyshire (from 1771); Samuel Greg's Styal, Cheshire (from 1784); David Dale's New Lanark (founded 1783 but developed and made famous by Robert Owen from 1800) and the Union Ironworks' Butetown in the Rhymni Valley, Glamorgan (from 1802). More impersonal were the several towns established by Victorian railway companies, but significant among model industrial communities built, with social facilities and to orderly plans, by well-motivated employers were Edwin Ack-

royd's Copley (c. 1847–53) and his Ackroyden (by (Sir) Gilbert Scott and W. H. Crossland, from 1859), both near Halifax. The most important and extensive example is Sir Titus Salt's town of Saltaire, near Shipley (by Lockwood & Mawson, from c. 1850). Among many lesser known instances are, all near Bolton, the Ashworth's New Eagley Village and Egerton, and (from c. 1840) Robert Gardner's settlement at Barrow Bridge. Also, and within a mile of Port Sunlight, there is the Bromborough Pool Village of Price's Patent Candle Co. (by Julian Hill, from 1853).

In their housing and their layouts these places did not depart from the utilitarian rows of urban terraces and grid plans. They merely improved on them, and open spaces were generally little more than adjuncts. It is true that architectural aspiration and picturesque siting may characterise rural model cottages, and that the achievements of Victorian improving country landowners working in a tradition with its roots in the 18th century have tended to be under-estimated in assessments of housing reform. Yet little direct comparison can be made between estate villages in an agricultural community and the problems of the towns. The historical significance of Port Sunlight lies in its unprecedented combination of model industrial housing, and on a considerable scale at that, with the tradition of the silvan suburb, in which greenery and picturesque effect form integral elements in spacious planning.

It is not known to what extent Lever may have been familiar with Saltaire and other precursors, though in his youth he must have known Barrow Bridge which, having been visited by the Prince Consort and Disraeli, enjoyed local fame, and undoubtedly he was aware of public-spirited Bolton industrialists and their benefactions. Moreover, his friend Jonathan Simpson designed some terraces of model cottages, built 1884–86 in the Haulgh, Bolton, for a trust established by Dr Samuel Chadwick, a noted local worthy. Remarks of the philanthropic industrialist Joseph Strutt of Belper, quoted by Samuel Smiles, anticipate Lever's concept of 'prosperity sharing' and must have touched a receptive chord within him: '. . . it would be ungrateful in me not to employ a portion of the fortune I possess in promoting the welfare of those amongst whom I live, and by whose industry I have been aided in its organisation.'[1]

When travelling, both on business and otherwise, Lever was a keen observer of architecture. On an early visit to Chatsworth he may well have seen the village of Edensor (rebuilt by (Sir) Joseph Paxton and John Robertson, 1838–42, for the sixth Duke of Devonshire) and he must have been aware of the massive programme of improvements carried out by the Chester architect John Douglas (whose firm he employed at Port Sunlight) on the first Duke of Westminster's Eaton Estate. He appreciated the beauties of English country towns and villages, and in 1887, just prior to the founding of Port Sunlight, a holiday in the West Country included visits to Dorchester, Blandford, Shaftesbury and Salisbury. It is believed that in the course of continental travel he saw Agneta Park, the model village of the Dutch industrialist van Marken at Delft, but at a time when Port Sunlight was already well advanced. Planned in the English manner of Nash, Loudon and Paxton, with buildings integrated in parkland, Agneta Park was begun just before Port Sunlight, and each village subsequently featured in the other's literature.

Accounts of journeys were published in the Lever Brothers house journal *Progress*, and that of his first voyage round the world in 1892 appeared in book form as *Following the Flag*. Here he recorded impressions of towns and cities, noting favourably such features as spacious boulevards or provision of parks, and, most important of all, his reaction to the then unfinished Columbian Exposition (World's Fair), in Chicago: 'For picturesqueness of situation, beauty and extent of buildings, arrangement, conception and general execution it leaves nothing to be desired . . . In addition to size which itself is always impressive, each building from a purely architectural point-of-view is well-conceived, duly proportioned and most admirably executed.'[2] The exhibition, held in 1893, initiated the 'City Beautiful' movement in America, giving, as it did, impetus and inspiration to revival of classical architecture and concepts of civic design. These left their mark on later developments at Port Sunlight as much as on Lever himself, no doubt reinforcing his belief in the virtues of good planning, with defined order to the townscape.

Housing erected in connection with the locomotive works of the Lancashire & Yorkshire Railway at Horwich, near Bolton (*c.* 1886) was criticised by Lever. He noted the opportunity wasted by building 'on the same crowded plan' as had prevailed around the company's old works in Manchester.[3] Views on living conditions were expounded in an address of 1898, in which he referred to the work of Lord Shaftesbury, and to having studied Charles Booth's *Life and Labour of the People of London*. Lever said, 'A child that knows nothing of God's earth, of green fields, or sparkling brooks, of breezy hill and springy heather, and whose mind is stored with none of the beauties of nature, but knows only the drunkenness prevalent in the hideous slum it is forced to live in, and whose walks abroad have never extended beyond the corner public-house and the pawnshop, cannot be benefited by education. Such children grow up depraved, and become a danger and terror to the State; wealth-destroyers instead of wealth-producers.'[4] Overcrowded layouts were condemned. '. . . there can be no reason why man should not make towns livable and healthy . . . just as much subject to the beneficent influence of bright sunshine, fresh air, flowers, and plants, as the country.'[5] As for flats, 'All tenement dwellings,' he said in 1907, 'flats, and such devices for crowding a maximum amount of humanity in a minimum amount of ground space are destructive of healthy life.'[6] Then again, 'I am positive, from all the statistics available, that the most healthy conditions of the human race are obtained where the home unit exists in a self-contained house, with the living rooms on the ground floor and the bedrooms on the floor immediately over.'[7]

'The picture of a cottage crowned with a thatched roof, and with clinging ivy and climbing roses and a small garden foreground suggesting old-fashioned perfume of flowers and a home in which dwell content and happiness, appeals straight to the heart of each of us, and there are few who can resist its quiet, peaceful influence for good.'[8] Though the word 'picture' is here to be taken literally, meaning a painting of the scene described, Lever's approval of a *beau ideal* cottage home is clear, together with his belief that 'Art and the Beautiful unconsciously create an atmosphere in which happiness and the virtues grow and flourish.'[9]

In seeking a site for the new soap factory begun in 1888, space for a residential village had been a prime consideration; Port Sunlight tenancy was, from the first, confined to company employees and pensioners and, in accordance with the theory of prosperity sharing, no realistic return on the cost of outlay was intended. In his speech at the banquet which followed the ceremony of cutting the first sod, Lever remarked '. . . it is my hope, and my brother's hope . . . to build houses in which our work-people will be able to live and be comfortable. Semi-detached houses, with gardens back and front, in which they will be able to know more about the science of life than they can in a back slum, and in which they will learn that there is more enjoyment in life than in the mere going to and returning from work, and looking forward to Saturday night to draw their wages.'[10]

NOTES

1 Samuel Smiles, *Self Help*, 1895 edition, p.216 (first edition published 1859).

2 W. H. Lever, *Following the Flag*, 1893, p.7.

3 *The Builder*, vol. 82, 1902, p.318. The reference was made in discussion following the delivery of his paper on *The Buildings Erected at Port Sunlight and Thornton Hough* to the Architectural Association.

4 W. H. Lever, *Land for Houses*, paper read before North End Liberal Club [Birkenhead], Tuesday 4 October 1898, p.5.

5 *Ibid.*, p.2.

6 *Visit of International Housing Conference to Port Sunlight*, 9 August 1907, Chairman's address, pp.8–9.

7 *Ibid.*, p.9.

8 Sir William H. Lever, *Art and Beauty and the City*, three addresses, 1915, p.6.

9 *Ibid.*, p.6.

10 *Messrs. Lever's New Soap Works, Port Sunlight, Cheshire. Full Reports of the Ceremony of Cutting the First Sod, and Proceedings at the Inaugural Banquet*, 1888, pp.28–29.

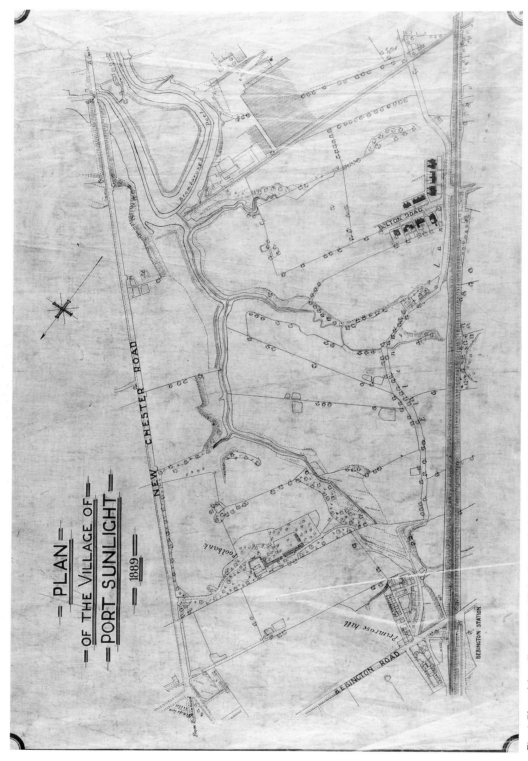

Fig. 4 Plan of the village, 1889. All that has so-far been built is part of the first group of cottages (William Owen, 1889–90) at what was to become the junction of Bolton and Greendale Roads. The rest of the site is mostly marsh, traversed by tidal inlets running from Bromborough Pool in the SE (top RH) corner; the slum housing is at 'Primrose Hill' near the NW corner

THREE

Planning and Development

Port Sunlight, named after the product that had so rapidly outgrown the Warrington works, was inaugurated on 3 March 1888, when Mrs W. H. Lever performed the ceremony of cutting the first sod. The site, in Wirral, had been chosen by Lever and William Owen after extensive searching. It allowed room for future expansion, was near a potential source of labour, and had facilities for road, rail and water transport. Bromborough Pool, an inlet of the River Mersey, provided a dock for the factory. There was also the advantage of cheapness, for much of the land was of poor quality—the site over which the village ultimately extended was marshy, and traversed by tidal inlets from the Pool in the form of muddy creeks. These followed roughly an E-plan, with a main channel (running north-south parallel with the river) and three western branches. The few buildings on the site included some insanitary housing near the NW corner (Fig. 2).

Fig. 5 Nos. 14–18 Bolton Road (Owen, 1889). The first cottages erected at Port Sunlight; destroyed in Second World War; commemorative plaque recorded a reproduction having been awarded a Grand Prix at the 1910 Brussels Exhibition

Fig. 6 The Dell, the only drained channel preserved as a permanent landscaped feature. Shows also Lyceum (Douglas & Fordham, 1894–96), formerly The Schools. Dell Bridge (Douglas & Fordham, 1894) is seen before cleaning and re-instatement of ball finials, 1987. Photograph 1980

Fig. 7 The Dell and buildings of 1892 on N side of Park Road. Shows, L to R: Part of Nos. 1–7 (Owen); Nos. 9–17 (Owen); part of Nos. 19–23 (Douglas & Fordham). Photograph 1966 (Royal Commission on the Historical Monuments of England)

Initially, *c*. 56 acres were purchased, of which 24 were allocated to the factory and 32 to the village. The factory, soon to be expanded, was completed in 1889, and in 1889–90 an entrance lodge and several blocks of cottages were built. The cottages, at the junction of what were to become Bolton and Greendale Roads, comprised 28 dwellings, and, like the factory itself, were designed by Owen (Figs. 4,5). A set of larger houses followed in 1890, and in 1891–92 came a further group of cottages, a shop (later Post Office) and the village's first place of assembly in the form of Gladstone Hall. Some or all of these buildings of 1891–92 were designed in limited competition, with those taking part including Owen, the Liverpool firm of Grayson & Ould, and probably Douglas & Fordham of Chester.

Further cottages, shops and public buildings were added 1893–97, thus completing the original village, which occupies the south-west corner of the later-expanded community. The layout was designed apparently by Owen, on the basis of a plan by Lever. It is outward-looking, with sets of cottages facing a railway and the factory. Then, turning in on itself, it encloses the south branch channel, drained and landscaped and spanned by a footbridge and known as The Dell (Figs. 6,7). Though this early portion remains the most attractive and visually satisfying area of the village, the problems posed by the topography were not fully solved. The curves of The Dell, and the adaptation of straight building lines to follow them, conflict with a basically rectangular concept of street plan. For the most part, the sets of cottages enclose small and awkwardly-shaped spaces at the rear (Fig.8), though one of these areas was large enough to serve as allotment gardens.

When work commenced, the extent to which the village might grow was not foreseen, and during a voyage round the world in 1892, Lever, according to his own statement, made a plan for future expansion. It seems that it was along the lines of this plan that development proceeded. In 1892 the land required for the scheme was not all owned by the com-

Fig. 8 An early superblock interior. Behind S side of Park Road (1893 and 1895) looking E to rear of Poets' Corner (1894). One similar early enclosure, and nearly all later ones, were large enough to contain allotments. Photograph mid-1890s

pany, and was acquired gradually, until the village reached its present size of *c*. 130 acres.

The dominating boundary lines are straight, comprising the factory and Wood Street on the south (this alignment dictated by a quarry tramway whose lines remained till *c*. 1912), the railway on the west, and Bebington and New Chester Roads on the north and east respectively. The extended plan continued the precedent of an outward-looking perimeter, with housing facing the two outer roads, and the buildings already erected opposite the railway being continued as the enfilade of Greendale Road. With an especially pleasing series of cottages, this presents an intentionally impressive public face to the railway, which in pre-Beeching days carried main-line passenger trains. Within, the layout was dictated by the channels, which penetrated into the heart of the site, and rendered the areas available for building awkward in size or shape or both. Again with a precedent in the earlier portion of the village, a system of superblocks (to use a later town planning term) was adopted, each with many blocks of cottages around its perimeter, and enclosing allotment gardens and areas where washing would be hidden from public gaze. Lever attached much significance to allotments and special ones for children were later provided. The very size of the superblocks minimised the irregularities of plan resulting from the curving roads skirting the edges of the branch channels. Among the routes of communication is Bolton Road, aligned on the mediaeval spire of Bebington church. (Other street names similarly have associations with Lever's native town). It was carried across the main channel by the Victoria Bridge, the erection of which in 1897 opened up for development the eastern portion of the site, where very little had previously been built. Intensive activity took place from 1898, and by the turn of the century well over 400 houses were in existence, with the perimeter almost entirely built up, and a start having been made in the centre (Fig. 9).

With legal rights having been obtained over them, the channels were filled in to above high-water mark, and cut off from Bromborough Pool by a dam 1901–02 (Figs. 10–13). It was intended that, like The Dell, they would remain as permanent landscape features, serving as parks and recreation grounds. They were, however, completely filled in and levelled, mostly 1909–10, and in 1910 a competition for a revised plan for the completion of the village was held, among students of the

Liverpool School of Architecture and the Department of Civic Design. The winner was Ernest Prestwich, a third-year student at the School of Architecture.

The central feature of the plan hitherto had been The Diamond, a space with two parallel sides cut off either end by sweeping roads skirting the branch channels—to the north Windy Bank and to the south The Causeway, then called Ellen's Lane. Except for Windy Bank (which, with Lower Road further north, remains the best illustration of housing following the line of a now-vanished channel) little of this layout had been built up by 1910, though the church (1902–04) had been sited at the east end of The Causeway (Fig. 10). Prestwich's plan involved the extension of The Diamond into a major formal element, the conversion of The Causeway into a second broad vista at right angles to it, aligned on the church, and the formation of roads radiating eastwards from the church. A formal square of public buildings, including an art gallery, was planned south of The Causeway, linking the church with existing buildings (Hulme Hall and the Bridge Inn) in Bolton Road (Fig. 14). The plan was, in its broad aspects, carried out, with revisions made by Lever and James Lomax-Simpson (son of his friend Jonathan Simpson) and with Mawson also probably involved. The site of the art gallery was transferred to the north end of The Diamond, making the axis an even more dominant element in the village than Prestwich had intended, and, with the other public buildings omitted, Bolton Road remained unsatisfactorily related to the formal layout. In 1910, a timber gymnasium, first built 1902, was moved from its site in The Causeway and re-erected next to the swimming baths (also of 1902) for the retention of which Prestwich had allowed. Both have since been demolished. The roads radiating from the church were laid out, and Lomax-Simpson designed cottages for them, but these were never built (Figs. 15–17).

Thus a classically-conceived *Beaux Arts* plan was imposed upon the partially-completed village, the commencement of which had been on very different lines—the lines of an informal and picturesque response to features of the terrain now obliterated. Except for The Dell, which still remains, the last section of channel to survive seems to have been in the angle between Bolton Road and Water Street. It served as children's allotments, and was apparently levelled in 1914, and The Ginnel built on part of the site.

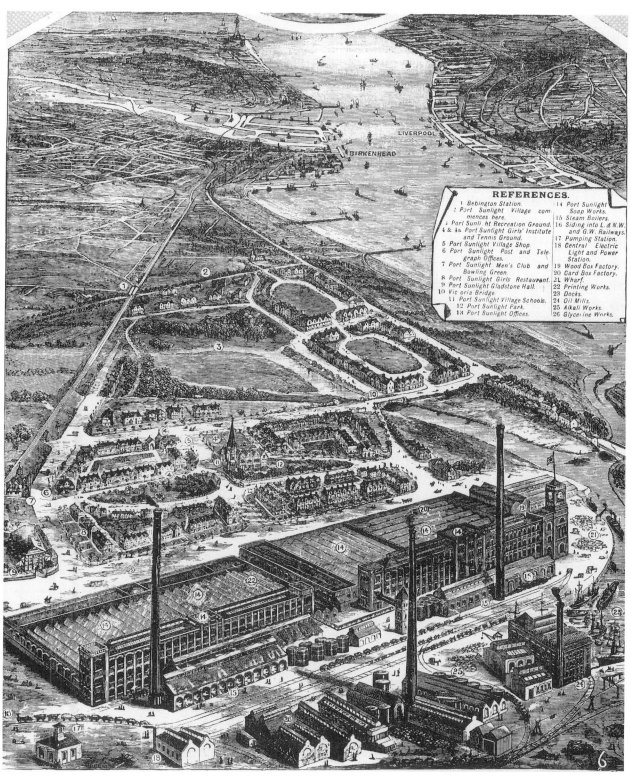

REFERENCES.

1 Bebington Station.
2 Port Sunlight Village commences here.
3 Port Sunlight Recreation Ground.
4 & 4a Port Sunlight Girls' Institute and Tennis Ground.
5 Port Sunlight Village Shop.
6 Port Sunlight Post and Telegraph Offices.
7 Port Sunlight Men's Club and Bowling Green.
8 Port Sunlight Girls Restaurant.
9 Port Sunlight Gladstone Hall.
10 Victoria Bridge.
11 Port Sunlight Village Schools.
12 Port Sunlight Park.
13 Port Sunlight Offices.
14 Port Sunlight Soap Works.
15 Steam Boilers.
16 Siding into L. & N.W. and G.W. Railways.
17 Pumping Station.
18 Central Electric Light and Power Station.
19 Wood Box Factory.
20 Card Box Factory.
21 Wharf.
22 Printing Works.
23 Docks.
24 Oil Mills.
25 Alkali Works.
26 Glycerine Works.

Fig. 9 Bird's eye view, 1898. In the foreground is the factory with its tall chimneys: to right, No. 1 Soapery (1888–89, Owen) with its corner belvedere tower and its wharf on Bromborough Pool; to left, extensions to No. 1 Soapery (1893) and No. 2 Soapery with offices (1895–96, Owen). Behind it can be seen the first stage of the village, built 1889–97 around The Dell. Beyond, the incomplete state is apparent, with the perimeter partly built up and the centre still largely open and crossed by tidal creeks. The main channel branches from Bromborough Pool and is crossed by the Victoria Bridge.

In the distance are Liverpool Docks on the R bank of the River Mersey and Birkenhead Docks on the L with, beyond them, New Brighton Tower at the tip of the Wirral peninsula (*Illustrated London News*, v.113, 1898, p.563, fig. 6)

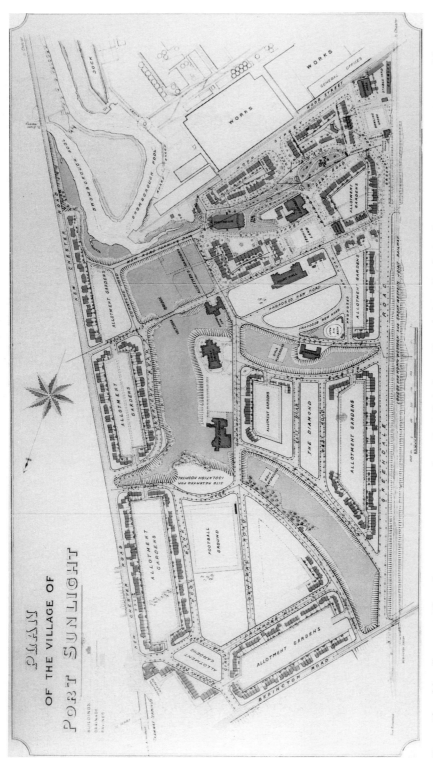

Fig. 10 Plan of the village, 1905. The earliest portion, 1889–97, encloses The Dell (the former S branch channel) at the SW (bottom RH) corner. In contrast, most of the rest of the layout is on the enlarged superblock pattern, with sets of cottages enclosing allotments. Most of the outward-looking perimeter has now been completed; some building has also taken place in the centre, planned around the channels. The position of the main inlet (with Church Drive Schools, Christ Church and the Bridge Inn along its W bank) is discernible, as are the N and middle branches. However, a dam cutting the channels off from Bromborough Pool, near the SE corner, had by this time permitted some of them to be partly filled in (W. H. Lever, *The Buildings Erected at Port Sunlight and Thornton Hough*, 2nd. ed., 1905)

Fig. 11 Looking W across the main channel, still tidal, with the Victoria Bridge (Owen, 1897) and Bridge Inn (Grayson & Ould, 1900). Immediately L of the inn are the gables of Nos. 1–8 Riverside (Grayson & Ould, 1896) and to the R, in distance, Hulme Hall (W. & S. Owen, 1900–01). One of the factory's tall chimneys is also visible. Photograph *c.* 1901

Fig. 12 Christ Church (W. & S. Owen, 1902–04) has joined the group beside the channel, now drained. Photograph *c.* 1905

Fig. 13 From similar viewpoint as Fig. 12, showing the channel partly filled in. Visible between the Bridge Inn and Christ Church is the Gymnasium (W. & S. Owen, 1902) on its original site in the middle of The Causeway. (Cf. Fig. 16). Photograph c. 1907

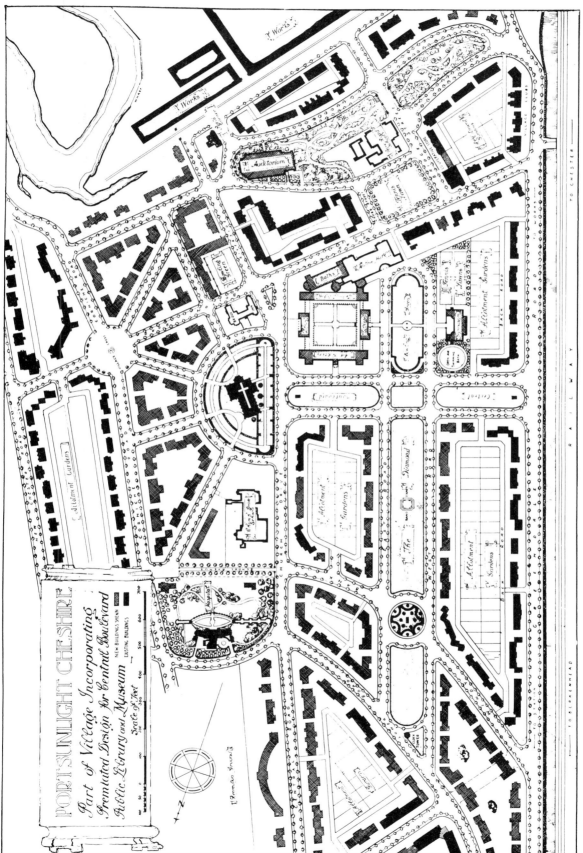

Fig. 14 Scheme for completion of village, 1910. Plan of the winning entry, by Ernest Prestwich, in the competition held after the channels had nearly all been filled in. Strong formality is introduced, with The Diamond and The Causeway as major intersecting axes; a square of public buildings (including an art gallery) links up with Bolton Road. This group remained unexecuted, as did housing shown on the site of the main channel, E of the church. At the N end of The Diamond (where the art gallery was in fact built) a clock tower was intended (Thomas H. Mawson, *Civic Art*, 1911, p.283, fig. 239)

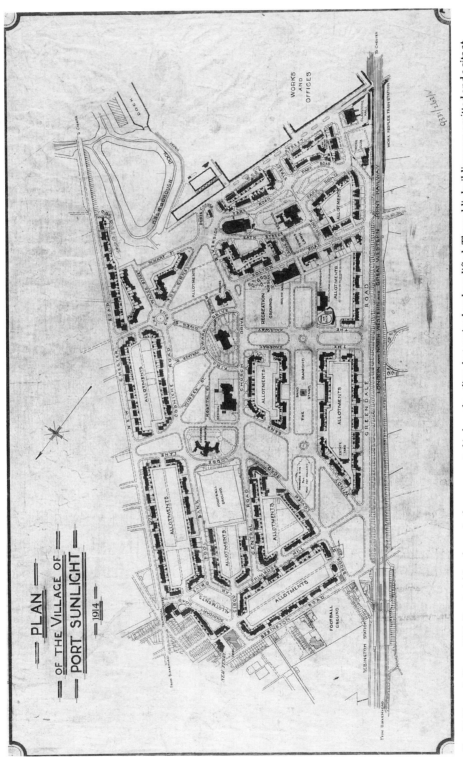

Fig. 15 Plan of village, 1914. Prestwich's scheme is shown executed in broad outline, but revised and modified. The public buildings are omitted and a site at the N end of The Diamond is reserved for the art gallery. Cottages have been built flanking The Diamond, though the roads radiating from the church are not built up. The earlier Gymnasium has been moved and re-erected next to the Swimming Bath at the SE corner of the intersection of The Diamond and The Causeway

Fig. 16 The Diamond, 1911. Looking N to the site of the Lady Lever Art Gallery. Roads have been laid out in accordance with Prestwich's plan; on the L is the resited Gymnasium (cf. Fig. 13) with Swimming Bath beyond; the small classical Bandstand (Lomax-Simpson, 1905–06) has also been moved in connection with the replanning, having originally been built further N; a circle in the centre of the intersection with The Causeway is where the War Memorial now stands. A new street lamp may be seen already in place. Cf. Fig. 54

Fig. 17 The Diamond. Looking N to Lady Lever Art Gallery (W. & S. Owen, 1913–22); cottages (Lomax-Simpson, 1911–13) in Queen Mary's Drive (L) and King George's Drive (R); cottages shown immediately to R of art gallery were never built (T. Raffles Davison, *Port Sunlight*. 1916, pl.2)

Fig. 18 Windy Bank. Looking E to Leverhulme Memorial and Lady Lever Art Gallery. The axial vista opened up by Lomax-Simpson, *c.* 1924–1926. On L the side of No. 10 Greendale Road, Nos. 1–3 Windy Bank, and part of No. 5, which links up with Nos. 17–22 Queen Mary's Drive

Addressing the International Housing Conference on its visit to Port Sunlight in 1907, Lever maintained that, 'The building of ten to twelve houses to the acre is the maximum that ought to be allowed . . . Houses should be built a minimum of 15 feet from the roadway . . . every house should have space available in the rear for vegetable garden. Open spaces for recreation should be laid out at frequent and convenient centres . . . A home requires a greensward and garden in front of it, just as much as a cup requires a saucer.'[1] Maintenance of the Port Sunlight saucers, initially entrusted to tenants, was soon taken over by the company, to ensure uniform neatness. The present free and open character dates from the 1920s, when garden railings were removed. With the gardens, the broad tree-lined roads, the communal open spaces (mostly on the sites of the channels) as well as the superblock enclosures, the overall density is well below the intended maximum of ten per acre.

Across New Chester Road, further housing was built on the Bromborough Port and Woodhead Estates, including work by Lomax-Simpson and Cleland & Hayward, but this remained separate from the village proper, and Lever formed an independent company to develop Bromborough Port. Within Port Sunlight itself, *c.* 890 houses had been completed by the time of Lever's death in 1925, few of them later than 1914. Some resumption of activity was probably initiated in his lifetime, for building work by Lomax-Simpson, immediately west of the art gallery, seems to be of 1924–26. It included the opening up of a short vista aligned on the gallery, involving the demolition of some earlier cottages, as well as the building of new, and the layout provided a setting for the later Leverhulme Memorial (Figs. 18, 19).

The history of the planning of the village ends with the building of a terraced garden and monumental arch. Of 1933–34 by Lomax-

Fig. 19 Leverhulme Memorial, in front of W entrance of Lady Lever Art Gallery. Completed 1930; designed by J. Lomax-Simpson; sculpture by (Sir) W. Reid Dick

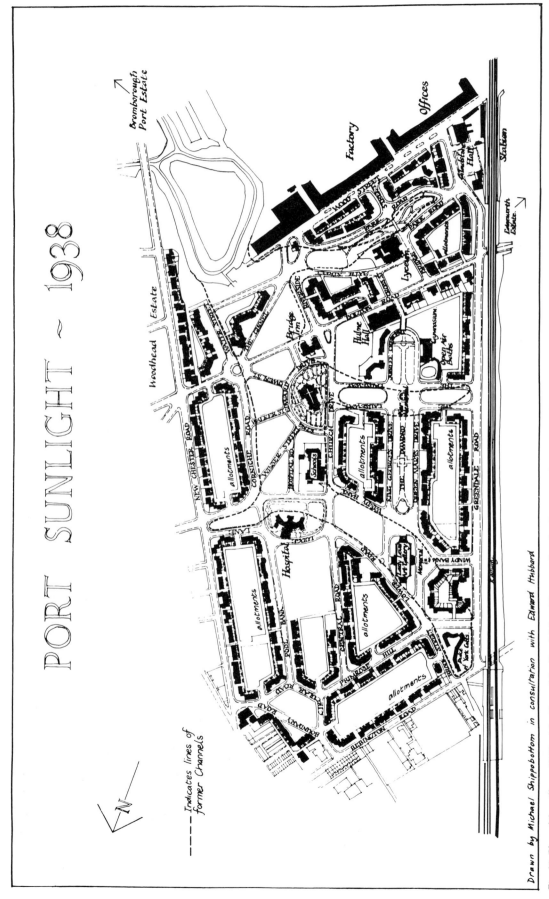

Fig. 20 Plan of the village, 1938, at the time of the first Jubilee. The art gallery has been completed and the formal vista cut through between it and the railway (see Fig. 19) involving demolition of some cottages (cf. Fig. 15); a formal termination has been given to the S end of The Diamond, and Jubilee Crescent erected in it; other buildings added since 1914 include Duke of York Cottages at the NW (bottom LH) corner; the War Memorial stands at the central intersection (Drawn by Michael Shippobottom in consultation with Edward Hubbard)

Simpson, these terminate the south continuation of The Diamond and help compensate for the absence of the public buildings of Prestwich's plan. Further cottages were also added in the 1930s, including Jubilee Crescent of 1938, commemorating the fiftieth anniversary of foundation (Figs. 20,21). Despite subsequent building work, sundry demolitions, war damage and changes in planting, there have been few major alterations in the appearance of the village since Lever's time. There are now 850 houses and, resulting from subdivision and remodellings, 72 flats and maisonettes.

In 1960 Port Sunlight was placed under the management of Unilever Merseyside Ltd (a Unilever services company renamed UML Ltd, 1968). In a modernisation programme, carried out by the Estates Department of the company, from 1963, cottages were admirably renovated (see p.30) and within the superblock enclosures allotments were replaced by garages and new gardens. Closure of some roads has banished unnecessary through traffic, and with Dutch elm disease having taken disastrous toll, a scheme of landscape rejuvenation was put in hand. This extended over a period of ten years, following the appointment of Pirkko Higson & Associates of Milton Keynes as consultants in 1978. Attention was given to resurfacing of paved areas, as well as to providing extensive and imaginatively varied planting, with tree planting concentrated in The Causeway and The Diamond. The roads are maintained not by UML, but by the local authority to whom inappropriate and obtrusive street lamps belong.

The most fundamental development within Port Sunlight's first century has been social rather than visual, for in 1980 cottages began to be made available for tenants to purchase. Protected by restrictive convenant as well as listed building and conservation area legislation, they are now sold on the open market, with occupation no longer confined to company employees.[2]

NOTES

1 *Visit of International Housing Conference to Port Sunlight*, pamphlet, 1907, pp.10–11.

2 Proposals for new (sheltered) housing on a site off Central Road seem likely to be implemented in 1996.

Fig. 21 War Memorial (Sir W. Goscombe John, 1916–21); in background are Christ Church (W. & S. Owen, 1902–04) and part of Jubilee Crescent (Lomax-Simpson, 1938)

Fig. 22 Cottage interiors, c. 1900 (W. H. Lever, *The Buildings Erected at Port Sunlight and Thornton Hough*, 2nd edn, 1905, p.24)

FOUR

Housing and Architectural Character

Until 1910, the architects most extensively employed at Port Sunlight were William Owen of Warrington (who was joined in partnership by his son Segar), Douglas & Fordham (later Douglas & Minshull) of Chester, Grayson & Ould of Liverpool, and J. J. Talbot of Wilson & Talbot, also a Liverpool practice. Between them, they were almost entirely responsible for the first stage of the village, of 1889–97. All were further employed in the burst of construction which followed, but at the same time, i.e. in and after 1897, a large number of other architects were brought in, each of them mostly designing a single block of cottages or, at the most, two or three. Of well-known London men, only Maurice B. Adams (two blocks), (Sir) Ernest George (Ernest George & Yeates, three blocks) and (Sir) Edwin Luytens and Ernest Newton (one each) were employed, and their work is not markedly superior to the rest. Also included were Lever's friend Jonathan Simpson, the latter's son James Lomax-Simpson, Edmund Kirby of Liverpool, T. M. Lockwood & Sons of Chester and Professor (Sir) Charles H. Reilly, together with—all of them north-western practitioners—W. Naseby Adams; F. J. Barnish; H. Beswick; H. Bloomfield Bare; Bradshaw & Gass; Cleland & Hayward; C. E. Deacon & Horsburgh; Garnett, Wright & Barnish; Huon A. Matear; Ormrod & Pomeroy; Pain & Blease and T. Taliesin Rees. A competition for cottage designs was held *c.* 1905 but in 1910 Lomax-Simpson was appointed Company Architect, and was responsible for most subsequent building work.

The era in which Port Sunlight was conceived was a golden age of English domestic architecture. The influence of William Morris and the Arts and Crafts Movement, and the refinement and sensitivity of Late Victorian aestheticism took their place in the new relaxed and confident 'domestic revival'. Free and eclectic adaptations of historical precedent prevailed, but particular impetus came from the styles of south-eastern vernacular building traditions as interpreted by George Devey and by W. Eden Nesfield and R. Norman Shaw. The 'Old English' manner of Nesfield and Shaw (to use their own term) and their followers was marked by picturesque groupings and varying materials artfully deployed. It is much in evidence at Port Sunlight, but inspired by the north-west rather than the Home Counties. Style and character were confined to external display, cottage interiors being utilitarian (Fig. 22). Advice on decorating and furnishing simple rooms, given in *The Sunlight Yearbook*, 1898, may perhaps have been directed at tenants. The backs also are plain, in contrast to the costly front elevations (Figs. 8,23,25).

No two blocks of cottages are identical, giving to the village the variety which is one of its endearing qualities. Owen's earliest cottages of 1889–90 are simple, with one block merely a plain brick rectangle with shallow oriels, though others are relieved by tile-hung gables. Greater ambition marks the work by Owen, Grayson & Ould and Douglas & Fordham which immediately followed. With much half-timbering, carved woodwork and masonry, pargetting (ornamental plaster-work), moulded and twisted chimneys, and leaded glazing patterns, it established not only a *penchant* for display, but also the high quality of external materials and detailing which was to be a hallmark of virtually all subsequent

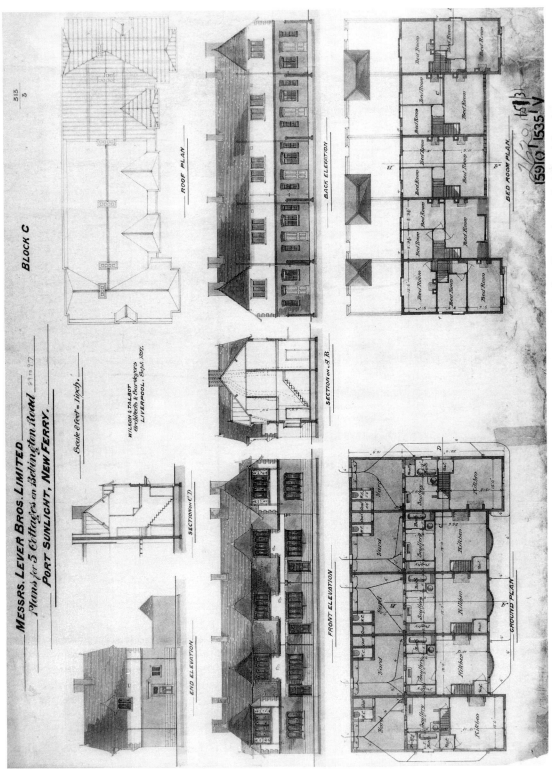

Fig. 23 Nos. 89–97 Bebington Road (Wilson & Talbot, 1897–99). Example of the three-bedroomed 'Kitchen Cottage' type. Architects' drawing

Fig. 24 Nos. 89–97 Bebington Road. Photograph *c.* 1902

building in the village. The early work is mostly hard and crisp, with, for instance, sparkling black-and-white half-timber set off by glowing Ruabon brick. The judicious and effective use of red pressed brick (not now universally accepted as an attractive material) is seen to particular advantage in the 1889–97 portion. In contrast are the softer and mellow textures of much of the 20th-century development. Especially apparent in the buildings of The Diamond, these illustrate the sensitivity to materials typical of the Arts & Crafts Movement's Edwardian phase. Though picturesque vernacular always prevailed, a further 20th-century element may, post-1913, be discerned in a neat and urbane underlying classicism, not specifically Neo-Georgian, but affined to it.

Inherent in the variety and elaboration was the danger of an exhibition-like quality, and Lever wisely abandoned an idea for groups of cottages in styles representing countries in which Lever Brothers had factories. Nevertheless a block in avowedly Belgian style (by Grayson & Ould) was built (Fig. 28).

In fact, the stylistic diversity is not as great as has sometimes been made out. Despite variations of form, design elements, detail, and the nature and colour of materials and finishes, the cottages are, with few exceptions, within the broad framework of vernacular revival idiom. This, together with a common scale, to say nothing of the guiding hand of Lever, provided a unifying factor, and made for harmony. The personalities of individual architects seldom obtrude. Indeed, it is difficult to distinguish from each other the respective works of those habitually employed.

One block of cottages (by Kirby, now demolished) was a reproduction of Shakespeare's Birthplace, and another (by Talbot) was closely based on the timber-framed Kenyon Peel Hall in Lancashire (Fig. 29), but such literal historicism was exceptional, and many of the blocks are of considerable originality and resourcefulness. Even the more inventive and fanciful are for the most part carefully and soberly done, with light-heartedness seldom tending to whimsy, and the general standard of design is consistently high.

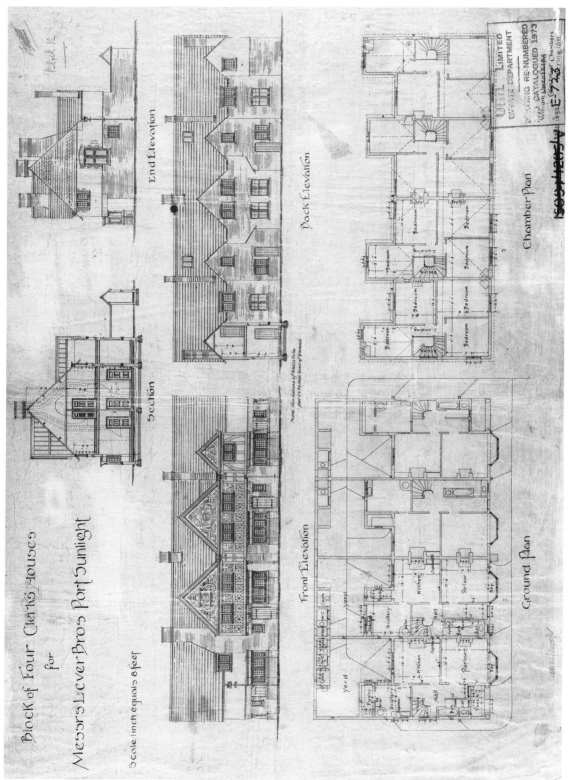

Fig. 25 Nos. 1–7 Park Road (Owen, 1892). Example of the four-bedroomed 'Parlour Cottage' type. Architect's drawing

Fig. 26 No. 5 Park Road. Pargetted gable.

Fig. 27 (below) N side of Park Road. Nos. 1–7 and
Nos. 9–17 (Owen, 1892). See also Fig. 7

Even so, Port Sunlight was never the pioneer in terms of architecture that it was within the social and planning fields, and early 20th-century advanced thought demanded a more restrained approach. In 1915 *The Builder* criticised cottages of 1906 by Bradshaw & Gass as 'over-featured', and in 1898 *The British Architect* had praised Newton's, built at that time, for their simplicity. Lever was aware that lavishness had drawbacks, commenting in 1902, that, 'The tendency at Port Sunlight has been during the last few years for our architects to become more and more elaborate in architectural design, and more and more extravagant in the use of costly building material.'[1] While approving the results of what thus could be done with unlimited money, he conceded the greater usefulness of achieving satisfactory ends with economy of means. Lever encouraged the use of new and cheaper building techniques elsewhere, but at Port Sunlight remained faithful to embellishment and traditional skills. Even the simpler of Lomax-Simpson's post-1910 cottages have delightful touches of ornament.

The blocks throughout the village range in size from two to eighteen cottages, though most consist of between three and ten. Many are of irregular plan, set back to form greens, ingeniously turning corners, or otherwise responding to site conditions and restrictions. Even if not progressive, architectural style accorded with good contemporary work. Similarly, domestic accommodation was to the accepted standard for working class model housing of the day, with only the provision of bathrooms being remarkable. Detailed planning varies from one house or block to another, but accommodation was of two standard types—the Kitchen Cottage, with kitchen, scullery and larder and three bedrooms above (Figs. 23, 24), and the Parlour Cottage with, in addition, a parlour and fourth bedroom (Figs. 25–27 and Fig. 7). A W.C. was reached from outside and it was noted that '. . . each house has the exceptional luxury of a bathroom.'[2] Some, though, had merely a covered bath in the scullery and most bathrooms were at ground floor level. Certain cottages had less than the standard accommodation; some of the four-bedroomed type were intended as clerk's houses, and a few larger houses were built for managerial staff.

Air raid damage was suffered in the Second World War, and under the direction of Lomax-Simpson, most cottages affected were faithfully restored or completely rebuilt in external facsimile.

In 1929 installation of electric lighting to replace gas had been begun. Unilever's modernisation work commenced in 1963 and continued in progressive phases for some twenty years. Not only did it bring garages (see p.23) but cottages have been renovated and, with sensitive skill, internally remodelled and refitted to modern standards. Some units were combined together and rear extensions have been added, but with virtually no alteration of frontages. Only the removal of redundant chimneypots, with just one remaining for each cottage, has marred the appearance of certain blocks, giving them a ragged look. Yet with the appearance of buildings preserved to an exemplary degree, and the layout little changed since the death of the founder, Port Sunlight offers unique opportunity to experience—and enjoy—a complete environment expressing late 19th- and early 20th-century social and visual ideals.

NOTES

1 W. H. Lever, *The Buildings Erected at Port Sunlight and Thornton Hough*, 2nd edn., 1905, p.7.
2 *Building News*, v.76, 1899, p.60.

Fig. 28 'Belgian Cottages'. Nos. 23–24 Windy Bank (Grayson & Ould, 1907). Built in Flemish style, of bricks imported from Belgium

Fig. 29 Kenyon Peel Cottages. Nos. 11–17 Greendale Road (Talbot, 1902). A close but not exact copy of the now demolished Kenyon Peel Hall, Lancashire

Fig. 30 Heritage Centre and National Westminster Bank, originally Girls' Hostel (Maxwell & Tuke, 1896). Shown when used as Lever Library; early 20-century hanging sign suspended from timber post no longer exists and this record of it may be compared with 1988 replacement (T. Raffles Davison, *Port Sunlight*, 1916, pl.17)

Fig. 31 Hulme Hall (W. & S. Owen, 1900–01). Built as women's dining hall. View shows another now vanished post with hanging sign. Photograph 1980

FIVE

Public Buildings

'Few self-contained communities are richer than Port Sunlight in social and educational institutions and in buildings to house them.'[1] Lever believed in providing a wide range of facilities, and gave encouragement to the numerous cultural, sporting and other societies and organisations which, from an early date (when the village was comparatively isolated from other amenities) have flourished. He criticised the Well Hall Estate at Woolwich, built for munition workers, because community buildings were lacking, and no such criticism could be levelled at Port Sunlight.

Some served dual or multi-purpose roles from the start; most have undergone changes of use, either as additional buildings were erected, or as requirements and social patterns changed, and there have been many enlargements and structural alterations. Similar architectural idiom marks both housing and public buildings, and a distinctive feature of many of the latter had been hanging signs carried by sturdy timber posts, well suited to the village (Figs. 30,31). In 1988 replacements of very different character began to appear. Though the standard of maintenance of the village as a whole remains extremely high, leasing of certain buildings to outside bodies means that immaculate perfection is no longer universal.

The Gladstone Hall (William Owen, 1891, Fig. 33) (the opening ceremony was performed by the statesman) was the first assembly and recreation hall. It also served as a men's dining room (planned with smaller rooms for male and female clerks respectively to take their meals) until canteen facilities were provided in the factory in 1910 (Fig. 34). Lever frequently lectured there; sacred concerts were held on

Fig. 32 Hulme Hall under construction. Photograph 1900

Fig. 33 Gladstone Theatre, originally Gladstone Hall (Owen, 1891)

Fig. 34 Gladstone Hall in use as men's dining hall, 1895. Unlike Hulme Hall, built ten years later, its kitchen facilities were limited and meals were not served—note luncheon baskets; paintings from Lever's collection adorn the walls and Hawarden Castle (Mr Gladstone's country residence) is depicted on the stage curtain

Sunday evenings and with stage facilities successively improved, it is now called the Gladstone Theatre. A functional and economical structure, it was described by Lever as, '. . . the most appropriate Village Hall we have. It is simple and unpretentious, admirably adapted for the purpose for which it was designed, and most suitable and appropriate for erection in a village.'[2]

Like the Gladstone Hall, a village shop (by Grayson & Ould) of 1891 resulted from the competition held in that year. It forms an appealing half-timbered termination to an attached row of cottages. It became the Post Office (Fig. 35) when, with the growth of the village, it was superseded by three shops (Douglas & Fordham, 1894) run by company employees themselves on co-operative lines. The first floor above them, later known as the Collegium, was built as a Girls' Institute—a club more educational than social. The block was destroyed by bombing and not rebuilt. By the same architects and of similar date is the Dell Bridge (1894) and the building known originally as The Schools (1894–96, enlarged 1898) (Fig. 6). This was also used for Sunday services before the church was built, and was available for other functions on week-nights. 'All the social work of the village,' said Lever in 1902, 'centres round these buildings,' which he described as those 'of which we are most proud at Port Sunlight, both architecturally and otherwise.'[3] It was the most important building to have been added to the village at its date, and forms a visual focal point in the early portion. Until the 1902 Education Act, the schools were run by the company, and after later becoming redundant for local authority requirements, the building served as a Staff Training College and was renamed the Lyceum. It has since been put to a number of various uses.

Two buildings of 1896, and of more domestic scale, completed the series of institutions provided in the early portion. The Men's Social Club (by Grayson & Ould), first called the Pavilion, has had several names and is now the Lever Club. After an attempt to run a Girls' Hostel proved a failure, the building erected for this purpose (by Maxwell & Tuke, Fig. 30) was put to a bewildering number of uses within a short space of time before being partially occupied, from 1903, by the Lever Free Library. The Heritage Centre now shares it with a bank. Anxious that employees' wages be paid into individual accounts, Lever first invited a bank to occupy the premises in 1919.

Hulme Hall (William & Segar Owen, 1900–01, Figs. 31,32), though from the start used for special functions and gatherings, was built specifically as a girls' dining room, to seat 1,500, and with kitchens for the service of meals. With canteens established in the factory, it served as a museum and art gallery, and Lever considered enlarging it for this purpose, before deciding to build the Lady Lever Art Gallery. It was at Hulme Hall that, by remote control and the use of a model, King George V, in 1914 laid the foundation stone of the new Gallery. Hulme Hall's stylish exterior is thorough-going and consistently done, even if no more elaborate than the Port Sunlight norm. However, moulded and enriched plasterwork marks high interior standards, and Lever clearly thought things had gone far enough when in developing his comments on extravagant construction (see p.30) he compared the Gladstone and Hulme Halls, to the detriment of the latter, remarking that it shows 'what can be done with unlimited money lavishly spent, which is perhaps the least useful lesson village architecture should teach.'[4]

The Bridge Inn (Grayson & Ould, 1900, Figs. 11–13,36) similarly shows no sign of stinting, but is simpler in treatment, and Lever seems to have thought that he here received better value for money. Named after the now-vanished Victoria Bridge, this idealised evocation of an ancient hostelry had dining, tea and assembly rooms, and a few guest bedrooms. It began as a 'temperance hotel' but after a couple of years a deputation requested that a licence be applied for. Although it was against his wishes, Lever complied, after having put the matter to the vote in a poll of village residents, and in 1903 the Bridge Inn was taken over by the Liverpool Public House Trust Co. This was a branch of Earl Grey's Public House Trust, a body which, with its circumspect serving of drink, was viewed with suspicion by the licensing trade. Having failed to secure adequate returns, the Trust relinquished responsibility which was, in 1905, assumed by a committee representing residents and Lever Brothers. A successor committee and a period of direct management by UML were followed by the granting of a lease to a brewery company in 1981.

More was undertaken in 1902. Reflecting Lever's concern for physical fitness, in that year William & Segar Owen built the Gymnasium and an Open Air Swimming Bath (Figs.

Fig. 35 Post Office, originally general store (Grayson & Ould, 1891) (T. Raffles Davison, *Port Sunlight*, 1916, pl.19)

Fig. 36 Bridge Inn (Grayson & Ould, 1900). Entrance (S) front, before glazing of verandahs and building of porch (T. Raffles Davison, *Port Sunlight*, 1916, pl.24)

Fig. 37 Hesketh Hall, originally Technical Institute (Talbot, 1902–03)

13,16). The former (later Boys' Club) was a weather-boarded building which, in accordance with Prestwich's plan, was in 1910 moved from its original site to adjoin the swimming bath. Both are now destroyed. Except for the church, the most notable building of this period architecturally is the Technical Institute (J. J. Talbot, 1902–03, now Hesketh Hall and home of the Port Sunlight branch of the Royal British Legion, Fig. 37). The cost was met, not by the company, but by Lever himself. By Grayson & Ould and also of 1902–03, are the large Church Drive Schools (built originally to supplement the Douglas & Fordham building, and leased to the local education authority) and the first stage of the Auditorium. This was an open-air theatre, its covered and fully-equipped stage with a Renaissance-style proscenium. Within a year or so the area was enclosed with canvas upon a light framework; this in turn gave way to a more solid structure, seating 3,000, but it was never a success, and all has been demolished. Also by Grayson & Ould is the Cottage Hospital (1905–07), now a private nursing home (Fig. 38).

Later, in 1913, came the Girls' Club (now Residents' Club) which Lomax-Simpson skilfully handled opposite the site which had already been chosen for the art gallery (Fig. 39).

Christ Church and the Lady Lever Art Gallery were built at the expense of Lever himself, and were his own special and personal contributions to the village. They express not a little of his ideals and philosophies. The church reflects his Nonconformity and his undemanding theology, combined with a love of mediaeval churches and of beauty and richness in architecture, and a desire for beauty and dignity in worship and liturgy. It was established as an undenominational foundation, of a sort difficult to imagine outside the special circumstances and rarefied atmosphere of Port Sunlight. In fact its antecedents were rather on the interdenominational lines more familiar to a later generation, with the services which were held in the Schools being conducted in rotation by Free Church ministers and the vicar of New Ferry, in whose parish Port Sunlight lay. In 1900 the vicar withdrew from the scheme, and a resident minister for the village—a Wesleyan—was appointed. It was in his time that Christ Church was built. Though remaining undenominational, it was vested by Lever in the Congregational Union of England and Wales, with the stipulation that future ministers be Congregational. This

was merely to ensure continuance and legal standing, but in 1972 Congregationalism took Christ Church into the United Reformed Church and it is no longer even nominally undenominational.

By William & Segar Owen, 1902–04, Christ Church (Figs. 12,13,21,40) is of great splendour and sumptuousness. The style is the Neo-Perpendicular of the late phase of the Gothic Revival. It is built of red Cheshire sandstone with Arts & Crafts touches in its conventionalised features and details. Resembling work by Austin & Paley, it has all the quality and shortcomings of the manner. The form is that of a parish church, with a long and fully-fitted chancel, providing not a hint of Nonconformity. Despite the remarkable size and elaboration, an even grander scheme was first designed which Lever, to his lasting regret, rejected.

A structure to mark his future burial place and that of his wife, coterminous with the church, was designed soon after. In the form of a loggia and known as the Lady Lever Memorial, it was put in hand following her death in 1913 and contains an effigy by Sir William Goscombe John (Fig. 41). After Lever's own death, his effigy, by the same sculptor, was placed beside that of his wife.

Lever, whose taste in sculpture was progressive, was on terms of friendship with Goscombe John, an exponent of the naturalistic 'New Sculpture'. He was responsible also for the War Memorial at the intersection of The Diamond and The Causeway, and it is one of his most successful works (Figs. 21,42). Lever conceived the idea and discussed it with him as early as 1916; models were shown at the Academy in 1919, and the completed work unveiled 1921. It was at Lever's instigation that, after other possible locations had been considered, the War Memorial was sited at the focal point of the Village—a position which, it had been tacitly understood, was being reserved for a monument to himself. The Leverhulme Memorial of 1930 was therefore placed axially between the west front of the Lady Lever Art Gallery and the short vista which had been opened up c. 1924–1926 (see p.20). With an obelisk designed by Lomax-Simpson and sculpture by Sir William Reid Dick, it is a fine and worthy work, but in Port Sunlight superfluous. *Si monumentum requiris, circumspice.*

The firm of William & Segar Owen was entrusted also with the Lady Lever Art Gallery (Fig. 43). This was designed in 1913 and built

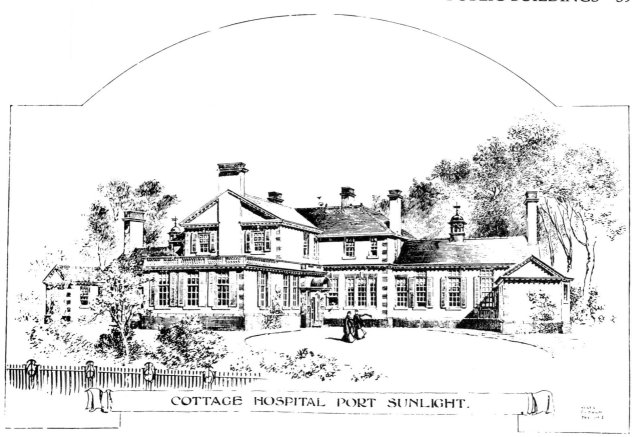

Fig. 38 Sunlight Lodge Nursing Home, originally Cottage Hospital (Grayson & Ould, 1905–07). Later extended (*Progress*, v.6, 1905, p.444)

Fig. 39 Residents' Club, originally Girls' Club (Lomax-Simpson, 1913)

1914–22, with progress being delayed by the Great War. Lever himself conceived the basic layout of the plan, and initially a library, with its own separate entrance, was intended. The structure is of reinforced concrete, then still unusual, if no longer pioneering, construction. The British Reinforced Concrete Company built the shell; internal finishes and features were built up in plaster (Figs. 44,45) and the exterior clad in Portland stone. A warm air heating system was integrated with the structure, and the plant, by Killick & Cochran of Liverpool, had facilities which either circulated cool air in hot weather, or may have been an early, unsophisticated attempt at humidity control.

A chaste and lovely treasure box of a building, it is an essay in scholarly and accomplished *Beaux Arts* classicism, and though the crowning glory of the village, it carried to extreme the departure into formality made by Prestwich's plan. Lever, who had been so impressed by the grandiose planning and architecture of the World's Fair twenty years before, continued to admire the classical movement in America; the comparable work of Professor Reilly and the Liverpool School of Architecture must have played a part in influencing him, and it was he who proposed the style and facing material. These were not, though, adopted without some misgiving, as witness a letter to Segar Owen: '. . . my suggestion of limestone and classical architecture must not be taken as ruling out all other styles. This was my first impression, but Mr Simpson [i.e. Lomax-Simpson] has expressed the view, and I think he is probably right, that it would be a little too hard for Port Sunlight Village, and that Renaissance [i.e. an Early Renaissance], with red Runcorn stone would harmonise better with the Village. Please therefore feel at liberty to adopt whatever style you think best.'[5]

Certainly Lever wished to restrict the scale and height so as not to overwhelm nearby cottages, and it is a measure of the architects' skill that they minimised and successfully integrated the great bulk, giving it horizontal emphasis and articulating the windowless walls (which themselves speak of Neo-Classical purity and restraint) by concentrating interest at four Ionic entrances (Figs. 17–19,43,46). Greek Ionic (most elegant of all classical orders) is also used within (Figs. 45,47). The plan has few major axes, and on paper is revealed as compartmentalised, lacking the spatial subtleties of true *Beaux Arts* expertise.

Lever's collection included architectural items such as panelling and chimneypieces, and characteristic of his taste and concern for education were 'period' rooms incorporated in the gallery. Most notable and intended as authentic furnished examples are the 'Kent' (Fig. 3) and 'Adam' Rooms, the latter designed by the decorator and furniture historian Percy Macquoid, shortly before Lever's death. He himself was deeply involved in the display and arrangement of the collection, and the gallery long remained a little altered period piece, enshrining the taste of the founder and his architects. Some modish and superficial remodellings of the 1960s have now largely been undone and in 1987 work began on sensitive and sympathetic refurbishment, and the provision of facilities to meet modern needs and enable the gallery to be better used and appreciated.

The Lady Lever Art Gallery and its contents was the most munificent of all Lever's public benefactions. It is a monument not only to his wife, but also to his love of beauty and to his fervent belief in the worthiness of art and its power for good upon the human mind and spirit.

NOTES

1 Viscount Leverhulme, *Viscount Leverhulme by his Son*, 1927, p.89.

2 W. H. Lever, *The Buildings Erected at Port Sunlight and Thornton Hough*, 2nd edn., 1905, p.10.

3 *Ibid.*, p.14.

4 *Ibid.*, p.12.

5 Lady Lever Art Gallery Archives. Transcript of copy letter. Lever to Segar Owen, 2 August 1913.

Fig. 40 Christ Church (W. & S. Owen, 1902–04) (T. Raffles Davison, *Port Sunlight*, 1916, pl.30)

Fig. 41 Christ Church. Lady Lever Memorial (W. & S. Owen, designed 1905, built 1913–14). Effigy by Sir W. Goscombe John, 1915.
The drawing by T. Raffles Davison shows the loggia before the addition of Lever's own effigy and before the addition of
railings and later infill of rooflights

Fig. 42 War Memorial (Sir W. Goscombe John, 1916–21). SW view. Upper group—Defence of the Home; lower group—the Royal Navy

Fig. 43 Lady Lever Art Gallery (W. & S. Owen, 1913–22), from SE. Photograph probably *c.* 1930. The foundation stone is immediately to the right of the entrance steps

Fig. 44 Lady Lever Art Gallery under construction. Main Hall showing bare reinforced concrete structure. Photograph probably 1918 (British Reinforced Concrete Engineering Company Ltd, *B.R.C. Structures*, 1927, p.227; British Architectural Library/R.I.B.A.)

Fig. 45 Lady Lever Art Gallery. Main Hall, showing original black and white colour scheme. Photograph probably *c.* 1930

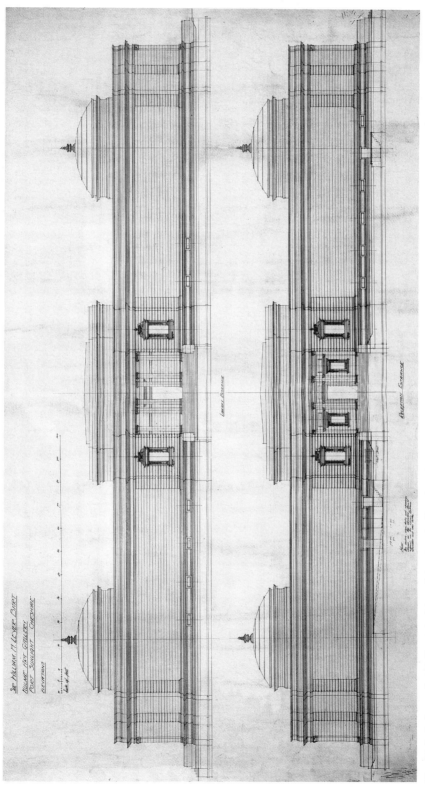

Fig. 46 Lady Lever Art Gallery. Architects' drawing for E and W elevations

Fig. 47 Lady Lever Art Gallery. S Sculpture Hall. Photograph probably *c.* 1930

SIX

Fame and Influence

Lever's flair for publicity made it unlikely that Port Sunlight would remain unknown, and from the very beginning it achieved fame.

As early as 1890 an article appeared in *The Illustrated London News*, followed by another in 1898; the visit of W. E. Gladstone to open the Gladstone Hall in 1891 focused public attention on the village; its buildings were regularly illustrated in the architectural press, and the illustrated text of Lever's address of 1902 to the Architectural Association on *The Buildings Erected at Port Sunlight and Thornton Hough* passed through two editions. In 1909 appeared W. L. George's study of *Labour and Housing at Port Sunlight*, followed in 1916 by the profusely illustrated *Port Sunlight*, by T. Raffles Davison, editor of *The British Architect*, a friend of Lever's, and a noted architectural draughtsman.

References and acclaim are to be found in books and journals abroad as well as in Britain, not least in the work of Hermann Muthesius, whose writings were largely responsible for making the significance of English domestic architecture known on the continent. In *Das Englische Haus*, he wrote, 'If one wishes to obtain a quick and accurate appreciation of the achievement of contemporary English house-building, there is hardly a more comfortable means than by undertaking a journey to the factory village of Port Sunlight near Liverpool.'[1] Elsewhere and more lyrically he noted, 'Port Sunlight will always be honoured with the highest recognition. For it is here that the gates of a new world were first opened; in place of the dismal appearance of utilitarian buildings we were shown a new vision; in place of the misery associated with the barren rows of workers' terraces we find joyfulness and homeliness.'[2] Reproductions of Port Sunlight cottages were erected at the international exhibitions in Paris (1900), Glasgow (1901), and Brussels (1910). That at Paris, in the annexe to the exhibition at Vincennes, was visited by the French president, and the Brussels block was awarded the Grand Prix in the social and economic section. The Glasgow cottages were, after the exhibition, presented by Lever Brothers to Glasgow Corporation, and may still be seen in Kelvingrove Park.

Inspiration was even provided for a musical comedy. *The Sunshine Girl*, by Paul Rubens and Arthur Wimperis, and produced by George Edwardes and J. E. Malone at the Gaiety Theatre in 1912, was set in Port Sunshine, the model village of a soap factory, and quotations from Port Sunlight architecture were included in one of the backdrops.

Visitors to Port Sunlight were, to say the least, encouraged. The first souvenir brochure for the factory and village appeared as early as 1891, and, although the largest and most sumptuous, it was followed by a long series of others, revised and kept up-to-date as the village grew and changed. In 1909 alone no less than 54,000 visitors saw over the factory, and it was largely to cater for sightseers that the Bridge Inn was built. Gladstone was but the first of many distinguished guests, who included Asquith and Lloyd George, as well as the Bulgarian Prime Minister, Field Marshall Sir George White, and the Crown Prince of Siam. Albert, King of the Belgians, went to look at the village in about 1903, while travelling incognito before succeeding to the throne. Above all, there was the visit of King George V and Queen Mary in 1914. The royal guests toured the factory and the village, and the king laid the foundation stone of the Lady Lever Art Gallery. The opening ceremony, in 1922, was performed by Princess Beatrice. The Prince of Wales (later King Edward VIII) paid a visit in 1931 and in 1934 the Duke of York (later George VI) opened the group of cottages which bear his name.

Of greatest significance were the countless

visits of labour delegations, industrialists, government officials and architects, of many nations. An early follower of the example set at Port Sunlight was Bournville, which had been founded near Birmingham in 1879 by George Cadbury, in connection with his cocoa and chocolate manufacturing business. Only in 1894, though, did extensive development begin, and, with W. Alexander Harvey as architect, it proceeded on the low density lines and with the concern for the overall environment which Lever had already established. In contrast to Port Sunlight, residence at Bournville was not initially confined to company employees, and a broader social spectrum was embraced. Moreover, the village was economically self-supporting, and its simple and informal style of architecture virtually established a norm. Between them, the examples of Port Sunlight and Bournville were of fundamental importance in furthering the garden city and garden suburb movement, in which Lever took a direct interest, and also in establishing the standards and styles of much of the best housing of the first half of the 20th century. The architects and planners Barry Parker and (Sir) Raymond Unwin were key figures in this evolution, and the influence of Port Sunlight (including the development of the superblock plan) is apparent in Unwin's own work.

The third industrial 'garden' village to be established was New Earswick, near York, begun 1902, with Unwin as architect. Like Bournville, it is not tied to the factory, and responsibility for it was placed in the hands of the autonomous Joseph Rowntree Village Trust, founded 1904. By then, the concept of the self-sufficient and independent garden city, as expounded by Ebenezer Howard, was achieving reality, with the building of Letchworth. It was commenced following the formation of the First Garden City Company Ltd in 1903, and the adoption of a plan by Parker & Unwin. Although he was to resign over policies of land availability, Lever was initially a director of the company. In 1902 the Garden City Association (formed to seek the implementation of Howard's ideas) had met in Liverpool under Lever's presidency. Howard was in attendance, and the conference members visited Port Sunlight. As C. B. Purdom noted, in referring to Port Sunlight and Bournville, '. . . the immense value of these villages as actual object lessons on a small scale of the practicability and commercial advantages of the proposals put forward by Mr Howard was incalculable.'[3] Inspiration for

the Housing and Town Planning Act of 1910 also owed much to them.

In 1910 a major and widely-reported international town planning conference, organised by the Royal Institute of British Architects, included Port Sunlight among its options of places to be visited, with notes in the conference handbook contributed by (Sir) Patrick Abercrombie. It was, moreover, represented in the exhibition, organised by Unwin and held at the Royal Academy, which accompanied the conference. A plan, photographs of streets, and drawings of Ernest Prestwich's planning proposals were shown, chosen by Unwin himself. *Beaux Arts* planning doubtless received impetus from the contemporary publicity given to Prestwich's scheme.

The eighth meeting of the International Housing Conference in 1907 (meeting in Britain for the first time) viewed Port Sunlight, and especially significant were visits of the French and the German Garden City Associations. Georges Benoît Lévy (Secretary of the French Association) and Bernhard Kampffmeyer (Chairman of the German Association) in their respective studies *La Cité-jardin* (1904) and *Aus Englischen Gartenstadten* (1910) were as enthusiastic about Port Sunlight as was Muthesius. Benoît Lévy had, in 1903, been sponsored by the Musée Social to make a close study of Port Sunlight and Bournville, and the English garden city and garden suburb movement did indeed inspire emulation on the continent, not least in architectural work by Muthesius himself.

Garden suburbs, owing much both visually and socially to the example of Bedford Park, differed from Letchworth not only in size but in being only social and not commercial entities. In a movement beginning with Ealing Tenants Ltd of 1901, many local schemes were launched under the auspices of Co-Partnership Tenants Ltd. Lever gave encouragement to a project at Warrington, and assisted plans for the formation of a tenants' company to acquire and develop part of the Bromborough Port Estate near Port Sunlight. Also nearby he created the Edgeworth Estate, exemplifying his theory that, for local authorities, provision of 'free land' for house building would be economic policy. More ambitious was the celebrated Hampstead Garden Suburb, of which Lever became a trustee, founded at the instigation of (Dame) Henrietta Barnett, and begun in 1906 to a plan by Parker & Unwin. Port Sunlight featured in its literature, and was illustrated by Dame Henrietta in lectures. The same tradition of cottage-style homes in spacious, healthy and pleasing surroundings was continued not only in the Second Garden City at Welwyn (from 1920), but in the best of the inter-war municipal housing estates, and it left its mark upon the post-1945 new towns. While reaction against, and demolition of, recent tower blocks continue apace, the qualities and importance of Port Sunlight and its progeny remain valid and admired.

Abercrombie, in his notes for the 1910 Town Planning Conference, wrote of Port Sunlight, 'as being one of the earliest of the self-contained "garden villages", which has exercised an enormous amount of influence on English and foreign planning, and . . . as a clear example of picturesque arrangement dictated by natural necessities.'[4] More recently Theo Crosby described it as 'a place we can learn from', and, with justifiable hyperbole, 'The first and only good housing estate in England.'[5]

NOTES

1 H. Muthesius, *Das Englishche Haus*, Berlin, 1904–05, vol. 1, p.199. Translation by Mr Alan Johnson.

2 Quoted by Nicholas Bullock and James Read in *The Movement for Housing Reform in Germany and France*, 1985, p.145.

3 C. B. Purdom, *The Garden City: A Study in the Development of a Modern Town*, 1913, p.25.

4 *Royal Institute of British Architects. Town Planning Conference . . .* , 1910, Members' Handbook, p. 102.

5 *Journal of the Royal Institute of British Architects*, 3rd ser., vol. 83, 1978, p.289, Theo Crosby, 'The First and Only Good Housing Estate in England'.

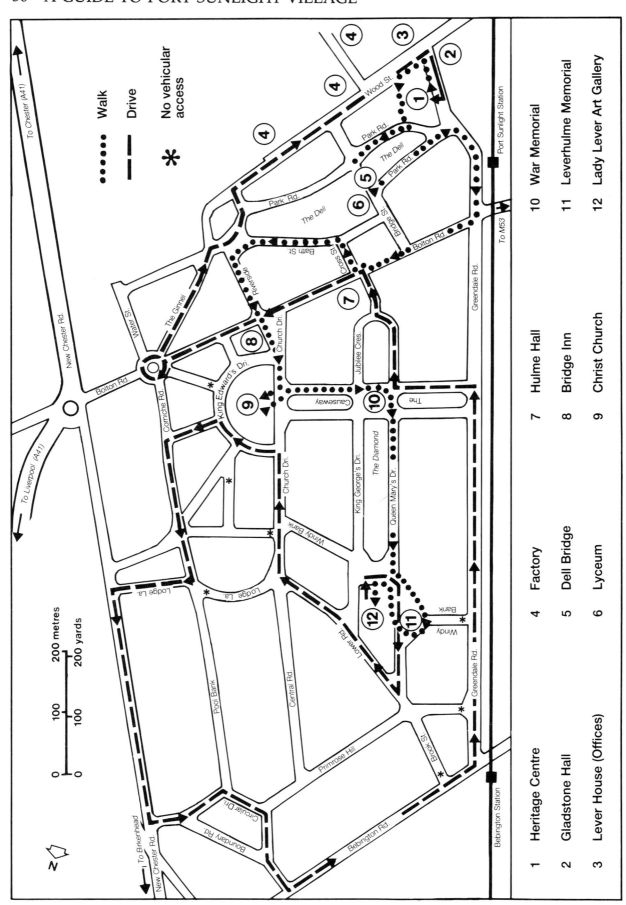

1	Heritage Centre	4	Factory	7	Hulme Hall	10	War Memorial
2	Gladstone Hall	5	Dell Bridge	8	Bridge Inn	11	Leverhulme Memorial
3	Lever House (Offices)	6	Lyceum	9	Christ Church	12	Lady Lever Art Gallery

Tours of the Village

Two routes are suggested: a Walk supplemented by a Drive, both being shown on the plan on p.50. In these tours L indicates 'left' and R indicates 'right'. Points of the compass are conventionally denoted: N,S,W,E.

WALK: HERITAGE CENTRE TO LADY LEVER ART GALLERY

Intended for visitors with limited time and includes the most important features and buildings.

HERITAGE CENTRE (the name dates from 1984) occupies the building erected for use as a Girls' Hostel, but for which there was found to be no demand (Fig. 30). Dating from the first main period of Port Sunlight's development, it looks across Greendale Road to the railway. (It is of 1896, by Maxwell & Tuke, designers of Blackpool Tower). Gabled front, typical of vernacular revivalism of village's early days in its half-timber and bright red brick; three different framing patterns for the four gables. Also a pargetted frieze containing figurative work as well as strapwork patterns. Wrought iron gates either end. MODEL on display shows present state of village and factory. Of several models known to have been made, two have associations with Lever's patronage of Liverpool University School of Architecture and Civic Design Department, but present one cannot be identified with either of these. Origin unknown, and it seems not to have been the one used in connection with laying the foundation stone of Lady Lever Art Gallery. Periodically updated in minute detail; has recorded demolitions, new building and the modernisation programme. Also substitution of diesel for steam trains and reduction of railway from four tracks to two.

Opposite Heritage Centre (but not its origi-nal site) is SILVER WEDDING FOUNTAIN (William Owen, 1899). Granite former drinking fountain, commemorating Mr & Mrs Lever's twenty-fifth anniversary. Behind the bowling green, R to L:

LEVER CLUB (a men's social club). Earliest part, originally called The Pavilion (Grayson & Ould, 1896) was built in connection with bowling green; it is the block nearest the railway. Half-timbered and formerly with a cupola; an early addition now forms part of adjoining station; prominent extension (1968) is an attempt at sympathetic half-timber.

A HOUSE with half-timbered gable is perhaps the ENTRANCE LODGE which William Owen is known to have built, 1889.

Gladstone Theatre, originally GLADSTONE HALL (Owen, 1891, Figs. 33,34). The first public building. Simple and economical; large window areas combined with unostentatious cladding of tile-hanging (quite rare in the village though a common architectural feature of the period) and half-timber; copper Art Nouveau commemorative plaque by H. Bloomfield Bare, a craftsman who had a studio in the village; later alterations by J. Lomax-

Fig. 48 Lever House (office building). Entrance Hall. NO PUBLIC ACCESS. By Owen, 1895–96, altered by Lomax-Simpson, 1913–14. The stairs probably belong to Lomax-Simpson's remodelling and their position is probably where Lever's glass-sided office had hitherto been; Royal Arms in mosaic floor (Lever Brothers having been appointed soapmakers to Queen Victoria, 1892). Photograph early 20th century. Later, to commemorate Port Sunlight's 1938 Jubilee, busts of both the Lever brothers were placed on the newel pedestals of the stairs

Simpson included addition of a storeyed porch housing a cinema projection room.

Beyond Gladstone Theatre is the FACTORY (see also pp. 65,66). Visible is the office building (LEVER HOUSE), its stone entrance front in ornate free classical (Owen, 1895–96, Fig. 48) and a more utilitarian higher block added in brick by Lomax-Simpson, 1913–14.

Walk towards factory, L into Wood Street and immediately L again for FIRE STATION (Fig. 49) or, as it more correctly proclaims, Fire Engine Station. Origin obscure, but probably mid or late 1890s;[1] in use as stables 1902 and became Fire Station 1906. A charming building; two wings at an angle; timber used for minor elements only, but predominates in character over brick and tile. As may be seen by venturing behind, is fitted into the otherwise useless space created by one of the first superblock enclosures (cf. Fig. 8). One con-

temporary and all subsequent such areas were large enough to contain allotments. Beyond Fire Station emerge into PARK ROAD, beside Nos. 2–4 (Owen, 1892). The block which was reproduced at the 1901 Glasgow Exhibition; two houses but an irregular asymmetrical composition; Port Sunlight picturesque vernacular at its most fully developed and sumptuously enjoyable; pargetted gable, heavily enriched timberwork (bargeboards, bressumer, brackets) and patterned framing. Down Park Road. On R, more houses by Owen; on L THE DELL. Landscaped fragment of top end of S branch channel, and the most readily recognisable survival of the tidal creeks. Pedestrian DELL BRIDGE (Douglas & Fordham, 1894, Fig. 6). The surface of the soft sandstone shows the effect of having been grit-blasted in 1987, but care was taken to protect the quality of Neo-Jacobean ornament, and ball finials were rein-

Fig. 49 Fire Engine Station. Probably built as stables, mid or late 1890s; converted to fire station (for horse-drawn engines), 1906. Photograph, with motorised brigade, 1927 (*Port Sunlight News*, v.5, 6 July 1927, p.201)

stated correctly. Grouping with the bridge is the LYCEUM (Douglas & Fordham, 1894–96, Fig. 6). Originally The Schools and also used for Sunday services. Free Jacobean style and equally free grouping; in scale with surroundings but has dignity and distinction appropriate to education and worship; varying elements subtly suggest the intended dual function (windows with Gothic touches but gables looking more domestic; corner bell turret). Diapered brick.

Cross bridge and up opposite side of Park Road. All houses on R are 1892. Nos. 19–23 (Douglas & Fordham, Figs. 50,51) are bigger than the standard cottages. The group is terminated by BRIDGE COTTAGE (No. 23). One of the largest houses in the village and occupied by Lever himself, 1896–97, while Thornton Manor was being rebuilt; end elevation sculpturally free and fanciful, with boldly projecting chimney stack and corner bay window. Facing material is limestone fragments (not flint). Nos. 19–21 have half-timber above a brick ground storey; beautifully detailed woodwork

(carved bargeboards and bressumers, with an inscription on that of 19, and small oriel windows with traceried lights); all three houses have decorative leaded glazing. Twisted brick chimneys are a standard pattern—built up of purpose-made bricks, they were designed by Douglas & Fordham for mass production by a Ruabon manufacturer. Nos. 9–17 (Owen, Figs. 7,27) is simpler, but the top-most block, Nos. 1–7 (Owen, Figs. 25–27), has two gorgeously pargetted gables; letters 'LBL' for Lever Brothers Ltd; a limited company was formed 1890; the four cottages are mirror images on plan, but differ in elevation either side of the gables. Park Road shows Port Sunlight exuberance fully fledged.

Less elaborate but equally pleasing is the half-timbered corner POST OFFICE (Grayson & Ould, 1891, Fig. 35), originally general store. R into GREENDALE ROAD to see that it forms part of a larger block (all same architects and date) and terminates a row of tile-hung cottages (Nos. 83–88). These are plain compared with Park Road's opulence, but even

Fig. 50 Nos. 19–23 Park Road (Douglas & Fordham, 1892). Bridge Cottage (23) in foreground

Fig. 51 No. 19 Park Road. Timber details

Fig. 52 Cross Street (Grayson & Ould, 1896)

Fig. 53 Bath Street (Talbot, 1895–97)

more economical were the earliest cottages built (Owen, 1889–90); among them are three blocks comprising Nos. 74–78, with tile-hanging and white-painted oriels. R into BOLTON ROAD where Nos. 2–12 (modernised and remodelled as Nos. 8–12), on R, are simpler still, without tile-hanging. No. 1 (Owen 1889) on opposite corner of Greendale Road, is one of the larger houses, as is No. 15 (Grayson & Ould, 1891), virtually a small villa, and the home of Edward Wainwright, who had been Lever Brothers' first soap-boiler at the Warrington factory. On R of Bolton Road, a post-war semi-detached pair, occupying site of Nos. 14–18, the very first cottages built, but which were destroyed in an air raid. Next, an open space on Bridge Street corner, is site of shops—Employees' Provident Stores and Collegium (Douglas & Fordham, 1894), destroyed in air raid. From here can be seen Nos. 8–14 BRIDGE STREET, a post-war reconstruction with frontage a close, but not exact, reproduction of the original (Grayson & Ould, 1894).

Continue down Bolton Road, On L, Nos. 17–21 (Owen, 1890). A block of three larger houses, occupied early this century by the minister, doctor and schoolmaster and probably built for professional men initially; the first attempt at any elaboration of treatment and materials, with some half-timber, though pebbledash predominates; now flats and maisonettes. Further on L, HULME HALL (W. & S. Owen, 1900–01, Figs. 31,32). Began life as women's dining hall; single-storeyed; Neo-Jacobean, of brick and stone, generously windowed; surmounted by large half-timbered gables with some enrichment. Hardly ostentatious by Port Sunlight standards, but the interior was designed with a view to quality, and it is the building which Lever considered excessively extravagant. On 20 Bolton Road, opposite, a tablet records impromptu visit by George V and Queen Mary, 1914. This cottage is end return of Nos. 1–9 CROSS STREET (Grayson & Ould, 1896, Fig. 52). Walling of small biscuit coloured bricks sets off red diapering, purpose made bricks and ornamental terra-cotta; French and Germanic elements, particularly French Late Gothic dormers; blank panelling; slight recession between shallow cross wings. View across bowling green (formerly a tennis lawn) to Lyceum; brick twisted chimneys belong to a Douglas & Fordham school extension of 1898. At this side of the building a rare survival—one of the hanging signs suspended from a post, such as were once a feature of the village. L into BATH STREET. The Dell, on R, is site of the vanished Auditorium. Nos. 3–33 (J. J. Talbot, 1895–97, Fig. 53). A splendid red brick group, strong, solid and rather Dutch looking; rhythm of gables—some large and freely shaped—and graceful white dormers; effect marred by unnecessary and under-scaled turret; some chimney stacks are panelled blocks, some clustered shafts. Comprising eighteen dwellings in all, this is the largest block in Port Sunlight and completed the earliest stage of the village. The first use of a boldly set back plan, here defining a green. (On the grass a pedestal carries a curious sphinx sundial, age and origin unknown). A courtyard enclosure is implied by two long ranges and one short, the form being determined by the curving boundary of The Dell. Plan is ingeniously staggered round several corners, lining up with the Cross Street block and, round to the L, with 1–8 RIVERSIDE (Grayson & Ould, 1896, Fig. 11). With this latter is seen a material not hitherto encountered—cement render—much used in the village from the mid-1890s, in association with brick, for simple work. Here, though, in a lavish front, with features including tile-hanging and heart patterns of other materials set in the plaster.

Open space beyond this point is the ghost of the main channel; even after the land was levelled, housing intended for the site by Prestwich never materialised. Some development had been stimulated on the further bank by the Victoria Bridge (Owen, 1897) which extended Bolton Road to link up with New Chester Road and what little had by then been built on the E perimeter. Shorn of its parapets and buried under Bolton Road, the eponymous Victoria Bridge still exists near the BRIDGE INN (Grayson & Ould, 1900, Figs. 11–13,36). Beside the hotel is a depression (now planted) retained to light the kitchen when the channel was filled in. On this elevation is a bold grouping of chimneystack, bay window and half-timbered gable. Nowhere else does half-timber appear, but dark-stained (not black) oak is much used. With colour-washed roughcast this provides the softer character and feeling for texture of materials typical of the early 20th century; may be contrasted with the harder feel and crisp detail of Hulme Hall. Though Victorian in date, Bridge Inn is more Edwardian in character; has much in common with garden city movement, not only in appearance, but in the ideal of health, purity and sobriety with which it was conceived. Large overhanging gables; U-plan with verandahs of cross wings cosily enclosing a forecourt; the verandah glazing is a later insertion, and the porch a tactful addition by Lomax-Simpson. No original internal character remains; removal of simple and appropriate genuine Victorian fittings continued in 1980s, giving way to heavy pseudo Victorianism; the fine dark-panelled dining room is altered beyond recognition. Large rear extension by the then Estates Department of Unilever Merseyside Ltd, 1964. This was generally well done with style and materials satisfactorily matched up, but the scale and proportions are not quite right; neither does it possess the expansive spirit of Merry England hospitality which the 1900 building so happily exudes.

So to Church Drive and CHRIST CHURCH (W. & S. Owen, 1902–04, Figs. 12,13,21,40). Of Helsby sandstone, ashlared outside and in. Lever Brothers own Building Department were main contractors; stone carving by J. J. Millson. Like Lever's other ecclesiastical buildings, the form is fully church-like, its Congregational origins belied by long chancel with choirstalls and a reredos; clerestoried nave with narrow passage aisles, double N^2 transepts; tower in angle of S transept and chancel. Conventionalised Late Gothic forms and details with strong horizontal emphasis externally. Squat proportions consistent with 20th-century late phase of Gothic Revival, also help to integrate the building into its village setting, as does the domestic character of the stone flagged roof. Fresh and lively departures from strict historical precedent include conventionalised tracery and the inward curving buttresses which break through the aisle roofs. The mouldings, also, belong unmistakably to c. 1900, rather than to the late Perpendicular of 400 years previously, which is the basic stylistic inspiration. Interior less successful though undeniably impressive; Gothic still done with enthusiasm, but mechanically and no longer with conviction. Not helped by indiscriminately rich furnishings (made by Hatch & Sons). Several stained glass windows by Heaton, Butler & Bayne; seemly but dull, in conventional late 19th-century style, very different from their excellent earlier work; all are Lever family memorials: E window (1909), N transept (1912), W window (1914) and S transept (1931), more striking and colourful than the others. In contrast are two brightly coloured and expressionist windows by the Hungarian Ervin Bossanyi (1950), one in either aisle. Worth a glance for its figure of St George

carved by H. Tyson Smith, is the Boys' Brigade Memorial (1931) at the W end.

Inscription of foundation stone (1902) in W wall faces inwards to the church, the idea of the external Lever burial place having by then been conceived. LADY LEVER MEMORIAL (so-called 'narthex' but more strictly a loggia) built against external W wall 1913–14 to a design which had been made by W. & S. Owen, 1905 (Fig. 41). Follows Perpendicular precedent more closely than does the church proper. Highly decorated—pinnacles, niches, etc., and rib-vaulted internally. Bronze recumbent effigy of Lady Lever (Sir W. Goscombe John, 1915) on black marble tomb-chest plinth; companion effigy of Viscount Leverhulme (Goscombe John, 1926) on a similar plinth; seated children originally at the base of the first plinth were repositioned centrally against the two; separate memorial bust of second Viscount Leverhulme (1949, probably by Sir Charles Wheeler); enclosing grilles by the Owen firm, 1935; nearby in churchyard are two attractive Barnish family memorials (a family with Lever associations) probably by Lomax-Simpson. Note exceedingly huge and heavy outer door of church; timber-framed lychgate (W. & S. Owen, 1905).

On leaving church, notice on opposite corner Nos. 1–5 CHURCH DRIVE with Nos. 5–7 THE CAUSEWAY (W. & S. Owen, 1901). Frontage to The Causeway is set at an angle, being intended as the beginning of a line to skirt the then still existing middle branch channel.

WAR MEMORIAL (Sir W. Goscombe John, 1916–21, Figs. 21,42) where The Causeway and The Diamond intersect. Its being 'a rare example of a war memorial which is genuinely moving and which avoids sentimentality' is an observation quoted more than once, but originating from one of the present writers. Granite structure adorned with bronze sculpture. Central runic cross encircled with a wonderful life-like group in the round (so much so that limbs and drapery overflow the plinth). The idea is 'defence of the home'. Soldiers guard women and children and a wounded comrade whom a nurse is about to tend; a seated woman cradles a group of infants, and a frightened little girl stands, guarded by her equally frightened but brave and defiant younger brother; a Boy Scout stands with the soldiers. Against the parapet of a surrounding enclosure are large panels in high relief, braking forward into the round, and representing the Anti-Aircraft (NW), Naval (SW, Fig. 42),

Fig. 54 NW junction of The Causeway and The Diamond. Nos. 13–17 The Causeway with 47–50 Queen Mary's Drive (Lomax-Simpson, 1911–13). Photograph probably *c.* 1914. Note modestly-scaled gas street lamp. Cf. Fig. 16

Fig. 55 Part of block comprising Nos. 31–46 Queen Mary's Drive, The Diamond (Lomax-Simpson, 1911–13)

and Military (SE) Services and the Red Cross (NE). Bas reliefs on parapet piers depict children offering wreaths for the fallen.

THE DIAMOND in its present form was laid out 1910 as the central boulevard of the re-planned village (Fig. 16); the name dates from when branch channels cut diagonally across at either end. Entirely built by J. Lomax-Simpson, 1911–13 (Fig. 17), with end blocks returning to face The Causeway. Early 20th-century use of gentler materials and exploitation of texture seen in rustic brick, colourwashed roughcast and woodwork less sharply defined than in earlier work; the effect would have been softer still when the oak was (as originally) left in its natural state rather than blackened (as now). In contrast may be seen, looking towards the railway, the end RH block—Nos. 18–34 The Causeway with Nos. 44–48 Greendale Road (Talbot, 1902) displaying the more insistent materials of earlier years.

Roofs of The Diamond include some which are of North Country stone flags; built into brickwork are fragments of random-looking masonry, implying, in the manner of George Devey, an imaginary centuries-long evolution (Fig. 54). KING GEORGE'S DRIVE forms RH (E) side of The Diamond and QUEEN MARY'S DRIVE the L (Figs. 54,55). Take the latter. Until the new trees reach maturity both sides will remain visible from each other. Theoretically impossible problem of reconciling grand formal planning with Port Sunlight's vernacular cottage architecture was solved with consummate skill. The centres of both sides of The Diamond are symmetrically recessed, opposite each other, thus imposing a cross-axis and implying a quadrangle, and both recessed ranges have three large gables. Though both sides are thus similar in general massing, within this discipline enormous variation occurs; both facing ranges differ from each other and neither is fully symmetrical in itself. Picturesque elaboration is as great as that which marks any of the earlier buildings of the village, with resourceful but unobtrusive differences of grouping, detail and materials; rustic brick, roughcast, stone, half-timber (including brick nogging), weather-boarding, etc. The far end of King George's Drive undergoes mutation from the character of domestic to public building, being terminated by the RESIDENTS' CLUB, originally Girls' Club (Lomax-Simpson, 1913, along with the rest of The Diamond, Fig. 39); transition made by an attached cottage block but which is separate from the main group and which, with a hipped roof, has a subtly more formal, classical feel. The club itself, with a pair of tall and dignified Jacobean stone bay windows, emphasised an important corner, opposite which the Lady Lever Art Gallery was about to be built; an unexpected touch of half-timber lurks round the far corner.

FOUNTAIN, at end of The Diamond, near art gallery. Lively sculpture by Sir Charles Wheeler, 1949. To the L (W) of art gallery, the LEVERHULME MEMORIAL, unveiled 1930 (Figs. 18,19). The designer was Lomax-Simpson, the sculptor (Sir) William Reid Dick—the same association as at Unilever House, London, of c. 1929–1931. An obelisk and its square fluted base are of polished granite and have something of the 'streamlined' styling of the period. Consistent in character is the crowning figure of 'Inspiration' which was shown outside Lutyens's British Pavilion at the 1930 Antwerp Exhibition; in contrast to its expressionism is a group of more realistic figures at ground level, representing Industry, Art, Education and Charity—ably composed and modelled but rather over-heavy in its symbolism and lacking the vitality of Goscombe John's War Memorial.

The setting of the Leverhulme Memorial is worthy of note, being the vista which Lomax-Simpson opened up on the W axis of the art gallery, c. 1924–1926. This brilliant piece of urban surgery involved curtailing rows of cottages in Greendale Road and Windy Bank. The latter range (Grayson & Ould, 1902) had been built alongside the N branch channel, aligned SE. Of it there remains Nos. 6–11 Windy Bank, with No. 6 refaced where truncated. A separate block of two was completely demolished. To balance the fragment and create a crescent effect, a new half-timbered block was built (numbered 5 Windy Bank with 17–22 Queen Mary's Drive). This repays careful study. Not symmetrical, though at first glance seemingly so. End groups of gables differ, in framing patterns as well as general massing; chimneys do not correspond; the more one looks, the more do subtle and entertaining variations and delightfully imaginative touches present themselves. Note tiny gabled windows looking inwards along the main roof. Also built as part of the scheme, 1926, are two pairs nearer the railway, almost facing each other and linked with their neighbours by screen walls containing shell niches—Nos. 2–4 Windy Bank (with two gables) and Nos. 1–3 (hipped and more formally conceived, Fig. 18).

For related work in Greendale Road see p.64.

Now, the great LADY LEVER ART GALLERY itself (William & Segar Owen, 1913–22). Main contractors were Lever Brothers' own Works Department (Bromborough Port Construction Company) who took over where the British Reinforced Concrete Company left off. All stone carving was by Earp Hobbs & Miller and J. J. Millson. The introverted mass is satisfactorily related to its setting, and, writing to Lever, Segar Owen described how their desired objective might be achieved. He referred to '. . . keeping a simple building with the entrances as the outstanding features,' and to '. . . long lines giving this large building a low dignified appearance [which] would, I think, harmonise with the Village, but at the same time stand out quite apart.'[3] (Figs. 17,19,43,46).

The classical language is spoken clearly and grammatically and a number of subtleties may be noted. The four entrances (all fluted Greek Ionic—the order used throughout the building) comprise three different designs, only the N and S porticoes being identical; all four entrance features project from the main block; those at the N and S are linked by quadrant re-entrants which read as the main corners of the building. These not only prevent harsh and abrupt edges, but form elements in the taut and concentrated end elevations—the S end has to exist as an independent entity closing The Diamond (Figs. 17,43). In contrast, portals on the long and otherwise featureless side elevations are strengthened by wider spacing and richer treatment of windows (Figs. 19,46). Included here possibly at Lever's own wish, these windows are emphasised by apron panels below, heavy framing and, particularly, by trophies above, depicting the arts. E and W entrances differ not only in plan, but in application of enrichment to the classical members (both pairs of windows vary in this respect also). Crispness of moulding and erudition of detail everywhere contribute to a classical *tour de force* such as seldom fell to the lot of an English architect to realise.

Large urns at S entrance were placed subsequent to completion of the building. Enclosure of protective railings (even here a regrettable necessity) of 1987 by Bruce Hyslop Ltd in association with the Property Department of National Museums and Galleries on Merseyside.

Skyline with central mass and at either end a shallow dome, expresses the internal plan; core is a high Main Hall of elongated H-plan (Figs. 44,45) lying between two Sculpture Halls (Fig. 47), both domed rotundas; smaller rooms are arranged round and between these main elements. Lever himself was largely responsible for the layout, and at his suggestion columns encircling the rotundas were, with excellent effect, coupled in pairs (Fig. 47). Eastern rooms were planned for the intended Library and on the W, one was provided for Masonic use (Lever was a Freemason). With a domed Reception Hall, the W entrance arrangements are grander internally than the others. All interiors are plastered, except for vestibules, where Hopton Wood stone of excellent ashlar finish gives a feeling of exceptional quality and solidity; inner roof lights of the domes are patterns of coloured glass. The larger galleries have fine enriched classical doorcases; all were originally such, but when the building was tampered with in the 1960s, those in the smaller rooms were destroyed and the openings reduced in size—something less readily rectified than the other alterations. A large basement room (called the Banqueting Hall) is inexplicably of bogus Tudor teashop style, some of its dark 'oak' being painted concrete.

Refurbishment and sympathetic remodelling to extend and improve facilities for visitors was undertaken in 1987–89 by the firm of Edmund Kirby (whose founder designed three cottage blocks in the village). An internal staircase was introduced near the SW corner and, at lower level, a special introductory display area formed, together with ramped access on the W.[4] The space is being used to house an exhibition exploring various aspects of the taste and collections of Lord Leverhulme, with a section about the building of the Gallery opening in 1996.

With their being integrated with the building, mention should here be made of the various period rooms which provide appropriate settings for Lever's furniture collection and which mirror the different styles employed by him in his own houses.

On display in the Lady Lever Art Gallery are firstly the works of art which Lever transferred from his huge private holdings to the gallery on its completion in 1922 and secondly the collections, mainly paintings, which he purchased in the last years of his life specifically for inclusion in the gallery. A few works were acquired after his death by the gallery's Trustees and some important paintings, notably by Rubens, were sold around 1958–61. Like many northern industrialists in the late 19th century

Lever began collecting paintings by rather conservative contemporary artists in the 1890s; he had, however, a special interest in art derived from his expertise in advertising soap—he incorporated in these advertisements reproductions of contemporary paintings having first purchased the originals for this purpose. His taste later became more eclectic to embrace 18th-century British art, particularly portraits, and Pre-Raphaelite paintings. He was one of the pioneer collectors of 18th-century British furniture and in this field the gallery's holdings are unequalled outside London. His enthusiasm for English 18th-century design can also be seen in the gallery's large and representative collection of Wedgwood pottery which also includes many of the original wax models commissioned by Wedgwood for execution as low relief decoration. Lever's taste in 17th- and 18th-century Chinese ceramics was equally catholic extending not only to porcelain but also to cloisonné and Canton enamels and to jades and hardstones; in these areas the gallery's collections are exceptionally rich with *famille verte*, *famille noire* and blue and white poreclain of great richness and variety. He was too conservative a collector to be interested in earlier Chinese wares and this conservativism is also apparent in his notable collection of classical sculpture of which he was probably the last major British private collector. Lever amassed much of his collections from other notable collectors—Thomas Hope for classical sculpture and Greek vases, Richard Bennett and Sir Trevor Lawrence for chinese porcelain, Lord Tweedmouth for Wedgwood, George McCulloch for contemporary paintings, James Orrock for 18th-century pictures and furniture—and the Lady Lever Art Gallery is probably the best surviving example of late Victorian and Edwardian taste.[5]

NOTES

1 Is not to be confused with a separate fire station at the factory (Owen, 1895).

2 Compass points are given according to traditional liturgical orientation, assuming the chancel to be at the E end.

3 Lady Lever Art Gallery Archives. Transcript of copy letter. Segar Owen to Lever, 23 August 1913.

4 Details of the work were supplied by Mr A. M. Macdonald of Messrs. Edmund Kirby.

5 Paragraph contributed by Edward Morris. A well illustrated Guide to the Lady Lever Art Gallery collections can be purchased at the Gallery.

DRIVE: LADY LEVER ART GALLERY TO HERITAGE CENTRE

A longer route, including features not seen in the Walk, and a selection of further noteworthy cottages.

Art gallery marks site of W end of N branch channel, the S and N edges of which are perpetuated by the curving lines of Windy Bank and Lower Road respectively.

Clockwise round gallery; in its NW corner, the marble L'OPPRIMÉ PRENANT CONSCIENCE DE SA FORCE (by the French sculptor A. G. Guilloux, 1913); into LOWER ROAD. On L, Nos. 15–27. Built 1906, before the gallery, by Professor (Sir) Charles H. Reilly, who induced Lever to take interest in the Liverpool School of Architecture and later to found the Chair of Civic Design. Shallow crescent of Mediterranean feel; continuous verandah with recognisably Reillyish details and round headed dormers with scrolly side volutes. Rather incongruous in Port Sunlight, despite Reilly's usual scholarly classicism being muted. Nos. 29–33 and 35–49 (two ranges both by Lomax-Simpson, 1906); set back forming a green, originally to enclose an established beech tree; some tile-hanging. Next, Nos. 51–59 with 66–72 CENTRAL ROAD (Lomax-Simpson, 1906, Fig. 56). A half-timbered corner block planned at an acute angle with a large gable as a focal point; though there are fewer tricks than in later work, the architect here also plays a teasing game of spot the asymmetry (e.g. placing of chimneys). On the opposite corner, LODGE LANE HOUSE (Lomax-Simpson, 1939–40), built as a Nurses' Home for the nearby Cottage Hospital.

R into CHURCH DRIVE, passing on L, grounds of SUNLIGHT LODGE (Grayson & Ould, 1905–07, Fig. 38). Former Cottage Hospital, entered from Lodge Lane, now a nursing home. Due to pebbledash, not immediately recognisable as Neo-Georgian—a style more usually associated with brick; sash windows (rare in the village). Original appearance changed by additions on S (W. & S. Owen) and N (Lomax-Simpson). Two alternative schemes for laying out the grounds were made by Mawson, 1906. On R is open space marking position of N branch channel; view across to Nos. 23–24 WINDY BANK (Grayson & Ould, 1907). Intended as Belgian style, as part of the plan (soon after abandoned) to build cottages representing countries where Lever Brothers had factories; the bricks were imported from Belgium. Large corner turret with conical roof; small stepped gable; a larger gable has straight sides but with steps implied by carefully graded brick; other brickwork of equally excellent workmanship, e.g. arch of doorway curved in two planes. On L, CHURCH DRIVE SCHOOL (Grayson & Ould, 1902–03). Loose and free grouping of diverse elements, mainly from 'Queen Anne' revival—the classical counterpart of Port Sunlight's 'Old English' and here used with equal irregularity of composition; the building stood near edge of the main channel—hence deep depression at rear, with playground remaining below present surrounding ground level. This, and an oriel window, may be seen by driving first L into KING EDWARD'S DRIVE and then round further into stump of a blocked road belonging to the now partly closed system, laid out 1910, radiating from the church. Back to and continue round King Edward's Drive, then L, with a view of the long panorama of CORNICHE ROAD, which ran alongside the main channel. L into Corniche Road. On R, Nos. 31–35 (one of the surprisingly few Port Sunlight buildings by Jonathan Simpson, father of J. Lomax-Simpson, 1899). A rather awkward flat-topped dormer, but also lovely floral Art Nouveau decoration in shallow pargetting. Charles Holden (later to achieve distinction with his London Transport and London University commissions) was working for Simpson at the time.[1] Is it fanciful to discern here the hand of an outstanding but still immature architect? Nos. 17–23 (1897–99). 'You're not trying to tell me this is by Lutyens', a friend exclaimed. Indeed, although one of the contributions to the village by the architects of national repute who were brought in c. 1897–99, there is little indication of the genius which had for some years already been apparent in the earliest of (Sir) Edwin Lutyens's Surrey houses and which had placed him in the forefront of domestic architects. Yet this is by no means a

Fig. 56 Nos. 51–59 Lower Road with 66–72 Central Road (Lomax-Simpson, 1906)

negligible work; porches and their roofs and the asymmetry of the tile-hung portions are worth analysing; Venetian windows give special character, but there is nothing of the mastery of materials which was his forte and which Lomax-Simpson later displayed to such good advantage in The Diamond.

R into LODGE LANE. On L, Nos. 12–20 with 69–75 POOL BANK (Grayson & Ould, 1898). Rather hard, both in its brick and in its 'Queen Anne' classicism, yet still rooted in Port Sunlight vernacular in eschewing sash windows and strict symmetry. Symmetrical portions to Pool Bank (with pair of bay windows) and Lodge Lane (with pediments) but informality is introduced with other blocks (including the linking portion of what is a staggered corner plan). Turn L into NEW CHESTER ROAD, leaving behind the exclusive tranquility of the village.[2] On the corner

Nos. 212–16 (W. & S. Owen, 1898). Another corner plan, here effectively generating unusually complicated massing; also exceptional is the range of motifs in the decorative brickwork set in rendering (the original now replaced with pebbledash); some tile-hanging; porch with a corner post (recognisable as an Owen feature); very exceptional for Port Sunlight, and possessing particular character, in rising in part direct from the pavement.

Continue along New Chester Road. Of cottages by well-known London architects, built in the late 1890s, the most successful are those of Ernest George & Yeates. By them, on L, Nos. 178–90, 1897. E-plan with a forecourt recessed between cross wings; roughcast, a pargetted gable and leaded glazing. Re-enter village proper at next on L for BOUNDARY ROAD and CIRCULAR DRIVE, but first see HESKETH HALL (former Technical Institute) on opposite corner. Now houses Port Sunlight branch of Royal British Legion. Begun 1902 by J. J. Talbot, the year of his death, and completed 1903, seemingly by Grayson & Ould. Pebbledashed entrance front with Venetian windows; only a modillion cornice gives any hint of the thrill in store round the corner in New Chester Road (Fig. 37); Talbot's usage of 17th-century domestic elements at its most opulently spectacular; two pargetted gables, an oriel with arched middle light, a big half-octagonal bay and a frieze with richly pargetted panels; equally elaborate brackets carry one gable; background of the plaster relief is now painted dark—no historical precedent for this, but is stunningly successful; dark painting out of cornice is less happy. View of Nos. 3–47 Boundary Road (Grayson & Ould, 1905). The frequently used device of two ranges at right angles set back to form a triangular enclosure; informal, with effectively placed gables; two shops link up with a row of cottages. Nos. 18–26 Circular Drive (Grayson & Ould, 1906). A generously scaled ogee cupola articulates the corner of this angled block and an arched porch nestles up against its lower stage. View L down PRIMROSE HILL. Of the straight roads in this N end of the village, this is the most attractive, with the character of cottage grouping enhanced by the gradient.

L into BEBINGTON ROAD and out of the village environment again. On L, Nos. 57–65 (W. & S. Owen, 1899); steep roofed end pavilions and dormers with curved pediments. Nos. 67–79 (Ernest Newton, 1899). Not recognisable as his work, but a simply treated elevation with clever use of overlapping symmetry (well worth studying); screens of turned balusters at the porches. Nos. 89–97 (Wilson & Talbot, 1897–99, Figs. 23,24). Some good touches (e.g. decorative panels incorporated with the main upper windows); overall impression is of steep hipped roofs, including dormers and larger half-hips, and of dark wood used for minor features.

L into GREENDALE ROAD—the long display facing the railway. On the corner, DUKE OF YORK COTTAGES (Lomax-Simpson, 1933–34, Fig. 57) built as pensioners' houses. The block sinuously wraps round a service court; public face has varying materials—stone, plaster, brick, half-timber, but used for successive parts of the frontage, rather than blended in close harmony as at The Diamond; some symmetry; the stone parts in Cotswold style—unique in the village; stone

roofs. At the far corner of PRIMROSE HILL is work by Lomax-Simpson, 1925 (Nos. 55–57 Primrose Hill and, planned diagonally on the corner, Nos. 3–6 Greendale Road). Dark rustic brick and of the neat, refined, underlyingly classical category, but still drawing on 17th-century domestic elements—timber mullions and leaded glazing, and, on the Greendale Road block, three shell door hoods. Nos. 6K–10 Greendale Road (Grayson & Ould, 1901) is the remainder of the block from which two cottages were removed in the course of cutting through a vista to the Art Gallery by Lomax-Simpson, c. 1924–1926 (see p.60). So well was the side of No. 10 refaced, with a bay window added, that no-one could suspect that amputation had taken place. KENYON PEEL COTTAGES—Nos. 11–17 (J. J. Talbot, 1902, Fig. 29). A close copy, though reduced in scale, of the timber-framed Jacobean Kenyon Peel Hall, not far from Bolton (demolished c. 1955). Shallow E-plan front with extruded corners; characteristic north-western patterned timber framing; patterned leaded glazing. Nos. 25–29 and 33–39 (both Ernest George & Yeates, 1901). Fresh and lively in an unassertive early 20th-century way; roughcast; massive Lutyens-like chimneys; Nos. 25–29 with three hips; the other has a long front, with unequal treatment of gables either end.

L into THE CAUSEWAY. On the far corner, Nos. 49–52 Greendale Road with 1–4 The Causeway (Grayson & Ould, 1901). The trouble with the dramatic spire-like roof which crowns the corner pavilion is that the lines of half-round ridge tiles cannot all continue unbroken—the feature is a good idea, but not fully resolved in terms of practical detailing. Before War Memorial, R into S end of Queen Mary's Drive. On L, view of JUBILEE CRESCENT (Lomax-Simpson, 1938, Fig. 21). Dating from the village's half centenary, and the last set of cottages built. Brick, some tile-hanging and weatherboarding. An extended, picturesque group of two separate blocks, one of them wholly irregular, the other with elements of symmetry and subtle variations; lacks the joyful and imaginative zest of earlier work and is rather inadequately integrated in its broad open setting. Continue round by the formal layout which closes the vista of The Diamond (Lomax-Simpson, 1933–34) and which includes BALUSTRADED TERRACE, GARDEN and ARCH. R by arch and L into BOLTON ROAD. Continue across site of main channel (which still remains as open space, though intended by Prestwich for housing) to

Fig. 57 Duke of York Cottages (Lomax-Simpson, 1933–34). Photographed during final stages of construction, probably 1934

roundabout (planned as a *rond point* for 'Village Cross'). Beside it Nos. 64–78 Bolton Road (W. & S. Owen, *c.* 1912). General character is Edwardian, with splayed wings a version of the 'butterfly' plan. Fourth exit from roundabout is THE GINNEL. Ranges on L comprise Nos. 1–35 (Lomax-Simpson, 1914). They include two forming a triangular green; difficult to analyse, so great is the diversity of materials (brick, roughcast, some pargetting in smooth-plastered gables) and elements (Doric columns, oriel windows, casements with glazing bars); overall flavour is classical, despite informal layout. In its neat, clean-cut way, the group is as imaginative and satisfying as the slightly earlier housing in The Diamond.

L across end of The Dell to POETS' CORNER.* On L, site of the demolished SHAKESPEARE COTTAGES. On R, Nos. 2–8 with 50–52 Park Road (Grayson & Ould, 1894). Corner turret with square spire forms pivotal

point for half-timbered front to Park Road and shorter return to Poets' Corner. Edward Ould's black-and-white expertise shows up the less convincing adjoining work at 38–48 Park Road (T. M. Lockwood, 1895). Rest of Poets' Corner elevation not fully resolved as a composition, but displays virtuoso use of brick and terra-cotta with quiet, neutral background of cement render; diaper patterning and, more particularly, windows integrated with blank panelling; terra-cotta used for pediments on doorways and cusped heads of panels and window lights.

R into WOOD STREET, one of the straight perimeter roads. Here the houses face the FACTORY, which, needless to say, has undergone numerous enlargements, rebuildings and other alterations since 1888. Early parts were almost entirely single storeyed (planned thus by Lever for efficiency) and original frontages remain. All of Ruabon brick; neatly handled, but with no special features, and contrasting with the beauty of the village.

On R, Nos. 27–35 and 37–47 (Grayson & Ould, 1895). Flemish character; brown brick; large stepped gables with brick spiral finials;

*Poets' Corner is now closed to vehicular traffic. Instead of continuing as far as The Dell, bear L at the end of The Ginnel and then R into Wood Street from where Nos. 2–8 Poets' Corner can be seen on R.

smaller curved gables built up in brick. Opposite these two blocks is the front of the original factory (Owen, 1888–89, Fig. 9). A four-storey part behind had a belvedere tower at the far L (SE) corner. A distinctive feature, this marked the spot where Mrs W. H. (later Lady) Lever cut the first sod inaugurating Port Sunlight. Sadly it was removed in 1970, and although a stump remains, nothing of the higher part of this historic first portion of the works is visible from Wood Street. Prominent landmarks seen from further afield in Wirral were tall factory chimneys, demolished in the 1960s. Next along Wood Street is the surviving front of an extension (also Owen) of 1893, with terra-cotta date inscription. Opposite this wall, a view R into BRIDGE STREET: on L, Nos. 16–22 (Owen, 1894). A sturdy block with two differing half-timbered gables and ashlared (sandstone) masonry playing an important part; brick twisted chimneys, thinner than Douglas's standard pattern. On opposite side of Bridge Street, Nos. 1–9 (Douglas & Fordham, 1893–94). No stone dressings; brick and terra-cotta used exclusively—for walling, coping of curly Dutch gables, mullions, traceried spandrels, cusped heads of window lights; brick diapering; roofs of corner turrets are rather Germanic in profile.

Continue up Wood Street. On R, Nos. 17–23 (Douglas & Fordham, 1892). Patterned wood-work, particularly bargeboards; pargetted gables, with swirling, almost Art Nouveau designs, combined with comparatively staid strapwork. Next on L, LEVER HOUSE with very long E and W office wings (W. & S. Owen, 1909), extending either side of the stone centrepiece seen earlier (see p.52). Until done away with in alterations by Lomax-Simpson, 1913–14, behind the entrance was the legendary Chairman's Office, from which Lever looked down through glazed walls at the long rows of clerical workers either side.

R into GREENDALE ROAD and return to HERITAGE CENTRE.

NOTES

1 Information kindly communicated by Mr Eitan Karol. A panel of similar decoration occurs at Nos. 30–38 Primrose Hill (also by Simpson, 1899, not included in the tour) identifiable as the Port Sunlight cottages on which Holden is known to have worked.
2 The frontage of cottages to this main road extends for more than half a mile and includes many by the several architects most active at Port Sunlight in the 1890s, particularly Grayson & Ould. One of their terra-cotta French dormers of Cross Street (see p.56) appears at Nos. 288–92 and a pair at Nos. 240–42 (all 1898). Also examples of the simple treatment of cement render relieved by brick chequer and diaper (mostly by Grayson & Ould and W. & S. Owen).

APPENDIX I

Demolished Buildings

This list does not include the many cottages which were repaired or rebuilt in exact external facsimile after air raid damage in the Second World War. It relates to the village only. For some reference to the factory see pp.65,66.

NOS. 14–18 BOLTON ROAD (Fig. 5). By William Owen, 1889–90. The first cottages built at Port Sunlight. Asymmetrical block of three with tile-hanging. A version was built at the 1910 Brussels Exhibition. Carried an Art Nouveau commemorative tablet, almost certainly by H. Bloomfield Bare, a craftsman whose workshop was in Windy Bank. Destroyed in an air raid and replaced by a semi-detached pair of different design.

NOS. 8–14 BRIDGE STREET. By Grayson & Ould, 1894. Destroyed in an air raid, and rebuilt with similar, but not exact, reproduction of original elevation.

EMPLOYEES' PROVIDENT STORES AND COLLEGIUM. Adjoined the above, on Bridge Street/Bolton Road corner. By Douglas & Fordham, 1894. Built for three co-operative shops with Girls' Institute (later called Collegium) above. Destroyed in air raid and not rebuilt.

SHAKESPEARE COTTAGES, Poets' Corner. By Edmund Kirby, 1896. Two cottages built as a reproduction of Shakespeare's Birthplace. Demolished 1938.

VICTORIA BRIDGE (Figs. 11–13). By William Owen, 1897, its name commemorating the Diamond Jubilee. Built to carry Bolton Road across the widest channel. Not demolished, but buried when the final stage of filling in the channel took place, c. 1909–10. Still exists beneath the road, near Bridge Inn. Parapet was re-used on a railway bridge in New Chester Road and re-appeared, in part, at the 1984 Liverpool International Garden Festival.[1]

FOUR COTTAGES IN GREENDALE ROAD, by Grayson & Ould, 1901. (Between present Nos. 10 and 11 and attached to present Nos. 6K–10) and FOUR COTTAGES IN WINDY BANK, by Grayson & Ould, 1902. (Continuing line of, and including two attached to, present Nos. 6–11 and a separate block of two). Demolished c. 1924 in opening up vista W of Art Gallery. Replaced by present Nos. 2–4 and 1–3 Windy Bank and by present No. 5 Windy Bank with 17–22 Queen Mary's Drive. Sides of present Nos. 10 Greendale Road and 6 Windy Bank were refaced. All by J. Lomax-Simpson, completed 1926.

OPEN AIR SWIMMING BATH. On southern corner of The Causeway and Queen Mary's Drive. By William & Segar Owen, 1902. Dressing huts, etc. were thatched. Closed 1971. Demolished 1975.

GYMNASIUM (Figs. 13, 16). By William & Segar Owen, 1902. Originally built on present War Memorial site. Was timber-framed and weather-boarded and thus not difficult to dismantle and re-erect when, in 1910 and in accordance with Prestwich's plan, it was moved to beside Swimming Bath in S end of Queen Mary's Drive. Had housed Arts & Crafts and Home Arts Exhibition, 1904 (emanating from H. Bloomfield Bare's studio in the village). Later used as retail store by Unilever's Macfisheries company, and was Boys' Club before demolished 1981–82.

AUDITORIUM, in E end of The Dell. Began as proscenium stage (by Grayson & Ould, 1902–05) and open air theatre. Defeated by the weather. Was almost immediately given an iron frame for canvas covering. A solid enclosing structure built 1906, accommodating 3,000 for large company and village gatherings; was also used as a skating rink. Unsightly and acoustics bad. Demolished 1937.

BANDSTAND (Figs. 16,17). By J. Lomax-Simpson, 1905–06. An open Ionic structure, first sited near N end of The Diamond. Moved to centre of The Diamond as part of the 1910 replanning. Demolished, probably 1932, when rose garden laid out.

[1] Inscribed stones from the bridge now re-erected opposite The Bridge Inn through the efforts of Gavin Hunter and UML.

Notes on Architects

The numerous architects who worked at Port Sunlight included many regularly employed by Lever elsewhere, and several firms and families stand out by reason of their influence on him, and the quantity and range of their contributions to the village.

JOHN DOUGLAS (1830–1911) was a pre-eminent provincial architect, receiving national and some international recognition. He studied under E. G. Paley of Lancaster and practised in Chester from c. 1860—as DOUGLAS & FORDHAM from c. 1884 and from c. 1897 as DOUGLAS & MINSHULL. Douglas's prolific output was largely ecclesiastical and domestic, and included much for the first Duke of Westminster on the Eaton Estate. His work was highly praised by Muthesius in *Das Englische Haus*. It is of individual character, and marked by sure proportions, careful detailing and a fine sense of craftsmanship and feel for materials. Styles which influenced him included local timber-framing, and this would have especially appealed to Lever. Douglas was the oldest and the then most famous of Lever's favoured group, and the one most likely to have been uncompromising on matters of style. His general influence is apparent in much of Port Sunlight's architecture; the firm was employed also at Thornton Manor and Thornton Hough village, but nowhere does Douglas appear at his most imaginative and idiosyncratic. DANIEL PORTER FORDHAM (c. 1846–1899) was probably the partner with whom Lever dealt, and the practice continued to be employed for only a short time after Fordham's premature retirement and death.

THOMAS HAYTON MAWSON (1861–1933) was arguably the leading landscape architect of his time. He contributed little to Port Sunlight, but on the strength not only of Lever's gargantuan gardens, but of his eminence and the family friendship which developed, cannot be omitted from any list of the professional designers. From establishing his own nursery in the Lake District, Mawson undertook garden and public park design, gradually developing a world-wide practice in landscape and town planning, and contributing to the literature of both subjects. Clients included Andrew Carnegie and the Marquess of Bute, and from 1905, numerous projects were undertaken for Lever, whom he regarded as his most important patron. Mawson tended to introduce formality and architectural treatment into landscaping, and in civic design shared Lever's admiration for grand and broad classicism, affined to the American City Beautiful Movement. Lever's abortive planning proposals for Bolton were drawn up by him. Three of his sons joined the firm, which became T. H. MAWSON & SONS, with EDWARD PRENTICE MAWSON (1885–1954) taking a leading role after training at the Architectural Association School in London and the École des Beaux-Arts in Paris. For a few years ROBERT ATKINSON (1883–1952)—later principal of the Architectural Association School—worked in association with the practice and was engaged on a number of Lever's commissions.

EDWARD AUGUSTUS LYLE OULD (1852–1909) trained under Douglas, and for a short time practised independently in Chester. In 1886 he was taken into partnership by GEORGE ENOCH GRAYSON (c. 1834–1912), already a successful architect in Liverpool. In the firm of GRAYSON & OULD, the former was the businessman, the latter the artist. The practice, which included domestic, commercial and some ecclesiastical work, is best remembered for its half-timber revivalism. Ould was an expert on black-and-white architecture, to which he would have been introduced in Douglas's office. He was responsible for the text in a book of examples, and it was to him and Jonathan Simpson that Lever entrusted restoration of the partly timber-framed Hall-i'-th'-Wood at Bolton.

WILLIAM OWEN (1846–1910) was articled to John Lowe of Manchester and served as assistant to James Redford. In 1869 he opened his own office in Warrington, where he developed a successful practice, undertaking domestic, industrial and commercial buildings. An accomplished draughtsman, he received training from the Bolton artist Selim Rothwell. He carried out work at Lever Brothers' Warrington factory, became a close friend of Lever's and in 1897 was made a director of the company. Owen was the first architect employed at Port Sunlight; his firm established the architectural idiom of the village, and was responsible for much of the early development. Two of his sons joined the practice—SEGAR OWEN, later Segar Segar-Owen (1874–1929) and GEOFFREY OWEN (1887–1965). Segar served with A. E. Street (son of G. E. Street) in London; trained at the Royal Academy Schools, and became his father's junior partner in 1898, the firm being styled William and Segar Owen. Geoffrey served with Dunn & Watson in London, before joining the family practice, and became a partner in 1912.[1]

JONATHAN SIMPSON (1850–1937) was Lever's closest friend, whom he first met at school. They shared similar tastes, and Simpson was a connoisseur and collector. He practised in Bolton, and his output was mainly, though not exclusively, domestic. Stylistically it was eclectic, with marked Arts & Crafts influence. For a while he employed as an assistant CHARLES HOLDEN, later to achieve fame for his work for London Transport and London University. Simpson designed only three cottage blocks at Port Sunlight, but would have had a powerful influence on Lever's taste.

JAMES LOMAX-SIMPSON (1882–1977) was Jonathan Simpson's son. He chose to add the hyphen into his name. He studied at Liverpool University and, on the recommendation of Lever (who was his godfather) became articled to Grayson & Ould. After setting up in practice in Liverpool in 1905 he occasionally helped with his father's work, as well as being employed by Lever. In 1910 he was appointed to take charge of the Architectural Department of Lever Brothers, and was made a director in 1917, but continued to undertake numerous personal Lever commissions. A talented architect, of great versatility, his work as Company Architect included overseas factories as well as Unilever House itself. His assistant in private practice, and then later his deputy at Lever Brothers, was BERNARD TAIT AUSTIN (1873–1955), son of H. J. Austin of Paley & Austin fame. ERNEST PRESTWICH (1889–1977), winner of the 1910 Port Sunlight planning competition, worked for a while under Lomax-Simpson at Lever Brothers.[2]

JOHN JOSEPH TALBOT (1871–1902) was a native of Bolton, where his father was a schoolmaster. He practised only from the mid-1890s till his early death, but in that short time regularly exhibited at the Royal Academy. Besides designing many cottages for Port Sunlight (where he resided c. 1896–97) Talbot worked for Lever at Thornton Manor. Elsewhere, commissions included some large suburban houses, and his work is marked by stylishness, quality of materials, thoroughness and careful detail. Had he lived, Lever (who attended his funeral) would doubtless have continued to employ him. c. 1896–1900 Talbot and WILLIAM GILMOUR WILSON (c. 1856–1943) were in partnership, practising in Liverpool and Bolton as WILSON & TALBOT. Wilson, who later developed a successful independent practice, had been an assistant to John Honeyman in Glasgow and to William Owen in Warrington.[3]

NOTES

1 Thanks are due for information and sustained assistance generously given by Mr Halsall Owen, son of Geoffrey.

2 No acknowledgements relating to Port Sunlight are complete without mention of Mr Lomax-Simpson, the last of Lever's architects to survive, and whose recollections of 'The Old Chief' and the building of the village, were an invaluable source of knowledge.

3 Mr J. Miles Broughton has conducted research concerning J. J. Talbot and W. G. Wilson.

Bibliography

E. W. Beeson, *Port Sunlight. The Model Village of England*, 1911

Walter L. Creese, *The Search for Environment*, 1966

T. Raffles Davison, *Port Sunlight*, 1916

W. L. George, *Labour and Housing at Port Sunlight*, 1909

Edward Hubbard, *The Work of John Douglas*, published by the Victorian Society, ed. Peter Howell, 1991

Edward Hubbard and Michael Shippobottom, 'Architecture' in *Lord Leverhulme*: Catalogue of an Exhibition presented at the Royal Academy of Arts by Unilever, to mark their Golden Jubilee, 1980. Details given of sources include references to almost all the numerous features relating to Port Sunlight which appeared in the professional and technical press; also cited are many items in the indispensable archive held by the Heritage Centre (formerly Lever Library) at Port Sunlight.

W. H. Lever [later Viscount Leverhulme], *The Buildings Erected at Port Sunlight and Thornton Hough*, 1902; 2nd edn., 1905

[Second Viscount Leverhulme], *Viscount Leverhulme by his Son*, 1927

Thomas H. Mawson, *Civic Art*, 1911

Edward Morris, ed., *Art and Business in Edwardian England: The Making of The Lady Lever Art Gallery*, 1992, reprint of a special issue of the *Journal of the History of Collections*, on sale at the Gallery

Nikolaus Pevsner and Edward Hubbard, *The Buildings of England: Cheshire*, 1971

Charles Wilson, *The History of Unilever*, 1954